GOING DEEP

WHY AUTHENTICITY IS THE ULTIMATE SALES STRATEGY

DYLAN CONROY

NATHAN PETTIJOHN

Copyright © 2025 Dylan Conroy and Nathan Pettijohn.

All rights reserved. No part of this publication may be reproduced, distributed, or transmitted in any form or by any means, including photocopying, recording, or other electronic or mechanical methods, without the prior written permission of the publisher, except in the case of brief quotations embodied in critical reviews and certain other noncommercial uses permitted by copyright law. For permission requests, write to the publisher, addressed "Attention: Permissions Coordinator," at the address below.

ISBN: 979-8-9887424-2-5 (Paperback)

ISBN: 979-8-9887424-3-2 (ebook)

Book cover design by Manny Loya.

Printed by Cordurouy LLC in the United States of America.

First printing edition 2025.

Cordurouy Books

665 Valley Dr

Hermosa Beach, CA 90254

www.cordurouy.com

❀ Formatted with Vellum

1

INTRODUCTION

Many describe sales as a numbers game. Conventional wisdom states that more calls, pitches, and proposals equal more deals. But the key to sustainable success isn't just about focusing on shallow connections as a volume game.

In advertising and media sales, I've generated over $50 million in revenue during my 15+ year career. This success wasn't because I chased every opportunity or jumped from one high-profile role to the next. I did it by going deep and building authentic, long-term relationships that naturally led to business growth.

Most sales books focus on deal-closing techniques. This book teaches you how to make deals come to you. The key? Building relationships so strong that sales become a natural byproduct, not the sole purpose. This book offers something different from traditional sales advice. While most sales methodologies focus on techniques to persuade prospects or overcome objections, "Going Deep" provides a transformative framework for creating business relationships that transcend transactions. In today's hyper-connected yet increasingly impersonal business environment, the ability to forge genuine human connections has become the ultimate competitive advantage.

This book offers a simple yet revolutionary approach to business relationships. Through my journey from boiler-room cold-caller to a trusted advisor for major brands, I'll show you how depth beats volume every time. You'll learn how to turn shallow connections into meaningful partnerships that generate consistent revenue without the pressure of hunting for new business.

THIS BOOK IS DIVIDED into three parts.

- *Part I* explores the philosophy behind deep relationship selling and explains why it is more effective and important than ever in today's digital age.
- *Part II* provides the strategic frameworks for building and maintaining deep relationships at scale.
- *Part III* gives you the practical tools and daily practices to implement everything.

Success depends on navigating human emotions and egos as much as understanding business metrics. You'll learn specific strategies that have worked for me, but more importantly, you'll develop the mindset needed to build authentic relationships in any industry.

I live in San Diego with my wife, Myla, and our kids, Teegan, Tennyson, and Tristan—the Triple Ts. While my friend Nate Pettijohn helped me write this book, every story and strategy comes from my direct experience. My goal is to help you transform your approach to sales by showing you how to build relationships that transcend traditional business boundaries.

The media and advertising world wasn't where I planned to land, but it was the perfect laboratory for developing this approach. Media sales allow you to build creative relationships unlike heavily regulated industries like finance or healthcare. We're not curing cancer, after all—we're in the business of influence, helping people market their services and gadgets to other people. It's the Russian nesting doll of capitalism, where success depends entirely on your ability to connect authentically with others.

In a world increasingly dominated by AI and automation, the ability to build genuine human connections is, I believe, becoming the ultimate competitive advantage. This book will show you how to master that skill. In today's business landscape, most professionals are drowning in shallow connections. You've got hundreds, maybe thousands, of LinkedIn contacts, email subscribers, and digital acquaintances. But how many of those relationships create meaningful value? How many would go out of their way to help you? How many truly understand your business and personal goals?

This crisis hides in plain sight: We're more connected than ever, yet we experience less genuine intimacy. The traditional approach of collecting as many business cards as possible and sending generic follow-ups isn't just ineffective—it prevents you from building the relationships that move the needle in your career and business.

Early in my career, I chased volume—more calls, contacts, and surface-level relationships. I was busy, but I wasn't building anything lasting. Everything changed when I started going deep with fewer, more strategic relationships.

Not only did my sales numbers improve dramatically, but my entire professional experience changed. Work became more meaningful, enjoyable, and less time-consuming in the long run. This isn't just about closing more deals. It's about creating a sustainable approach to business development that builds real value over time instead of constantly chasing the next transaction. It's about transforming the very nature of your professional relationships from transactional to meaningful.

PART I
THE PHILOSOPHY

CHAPTER 1

What does "going deep" even mean?

When I was in the early phases of setting up the revenue channel at Social Standard, a Nashville-based influencer marketing agency, I was trying not to burden the company with excessive travel expenses when I was out of town for meetings. One morning, as I was waking up in some crummy hotel in LA and getting ready to go on a run, I got a LinkedIn notification that a connection of mine, Jayson, had started a new job at Adobe. Immediately, I reached out to him in a direct message and said, "Hey, congratulations! I am stoked to see that you're at this new job. Here's a bit about what I do. Would love to meet up." Since then, he's explained why he even replied to my initial outreach. I didn't know Jayson personally, but we somehow connected on LinkedIn. When I looked at our LinkedIn history, we had connected back in 2012, even though he started that particular job at Adobe much later than that.

Jayson said that when he looked at my LinkedIn profile,

we had so many connections in common (over a hundred) that he would have felt guilty if he didn't get back to me. He said he worried it would get back to our associated mutual network if he blew me off. So he responded to me, and I offered to fly up to San Francisco and have lunch with him at the Adobe headquarters. I got on a plane quickly and made that happen, and within a few days after my initial outreach, we met in person.

I didn't have high expectations for that first meeting. After all, isn't Adobe the company that makes that PDF thing called Acrobat? I did not know what I was in for.

On the day of our meeting, I pulled up to Adobe's San Francisco headquarters—an imposing glass building that seemed to reflect the city's tech ambitions. Polished concrete and minimalist furniture filled the lobby, and giant screens showcased vivid imagery created with Adobe's software. I signed in at a sleek digital kiosk, took a visitor badge, and waited, feeling distinctly underdressed in my standard business casual attire.

After a few minutes, Jayson, my contact and lunch escort, appeared in the lobby. He wore his hip standard-issue sneakers, jeans, and a black T-shirt, which I later learned was his ongoing wardrobe style. "Welcome to Adobe," he said with a firm but not aggressive handshake—confident, but not trying to prove anything.

We went through one of those typical Silicon Valley lunchrooms where you could order anything you wanted to eat. The space buzzed with creative energy—designers with colorful hair and tattoos mixed with business types; everyone engaged in animated conversations about projects and deadlines.

"So," Jayson said as we sat down with our food, "what exactly does The Social Standard do with influencers?"

I launched into my rehearsed spiel, yet his engaged listening made me pause and adjust my direction. Instead of talking about metrics and conversion rates, I asked, "What are you guys trying to accomplish that isn't working right now?"

That simple question changed everything. Jayson leaned forward, coffee in hand, and began sharing their genuine challenges with reaching younger creators. "We've got the best creative tools in the world," he said, "but we're struggling to connect with the next generation who are building their careers on platforms that didn't even exist when we started."

For the next hour, we didn't talk about deliverables or costs. We spoke about creative people and how they work. We discussed the challenges of staying relevant in a rapidly changing digital landscape. Somewhere in that conversation, we stopped being potential business partners and started becoming actual friends.

Walking out of Adobe that day, I knew something significant had happened, though I couldn't yet see where it would lead. The meeting perfectly embodied what I now understand as the foundation of deep relationship building —I'd gone in curious rather than desperate, interested in his challenges rather than focused on my solution. We found genuine common ground between us that transcended the immediate business opportunity. I didn't know then that this lunch would be the first step in an eight-year journey to generate millions in revenue and culminate in joint family vacations. It all started not with a brilliant pitch but with a genuine connection over corporate cafeteria food.

LinkedIn notifications about connections starting new positions are a great signal anyone can take advantage of, even if (or especially if) you aren't hankering for an immediate quid pro quo. Just congratulating and cheerleading for people's success is benevolent enough on its own, and sometimes, it can result in going deeper. A one-to-one sniper rifle approach (which I will dive into in more detail in Chapter 4), when you see your contacts and your network moving around to new gigs, that is a great time to hit them up because they have a fresh start, and they're ready to get to work and make things happen—and bringing in new partnerships right out of the gate is a solid way to do that and help you both win. So that's how Jayson and I first met, and for the eight years after that, Adobe was one of my biggest clients.

My approach to sales boils down to the question: How do you go deep with a client? The truth is that you always have to start at the surface level. Jayson and I got together for a few more initial meetings, smoked cigars, and spent time together. Two years later, we took vacations with our wives and kids.

Our first trip was a follow-up to our activations at VidCon, which is in Anaheim. We planned to have our families meet each other for the first time at Disneyland right after VidCon. After traveling with Jayson and his family and getting to know them well over the years, his wife often harkens back to that initial trip as if she had been annoyed at the Disneyland plan. She was upset that they had to go along with a vendor relationship. He explained why he was doing that, but she was not a fan of hanging out with some random family at Disneyland for the first time. The cool part was that our kids hit it off and became friendly during that trip, as did our wives. And by the end of the journey, having spent time at dinners and hanging out at rides for a couple of days, it set the framework for us to do more stuff like that over the years.

We all went to Cancun, Mexico, together on three occasions. Shampa and Jayson are big fans of the Grateful Dead, and they have this concert down there called "Playing in the Sand," which is basically the Grateful Dead with John Mayer. It's always at an all-inclusive resort, and we joined them three years in a row, traveling down to Mexico for three nights of concerts with their favorite band of all time, getting better rooms each time at better hotels.

Before our third trip to Mexico, I wanted to find a way to provide some value. I couldn't just upgrade their room or make the trip more expensive and exciting simply by spending more money. The thing that I could do that money couldn't buy, so to speak, was reach out to John Mayer's management company before we went down on the trip.

I was sitting in my home office, staring at my email draft. The message to Irving Azoff Entertainment felt like a long shot—who was I to request special access to one of the biggest stars in music? I hesitated before hitting send, then reminded myself that the worst they could say was no.

To my surprise, they responded within hours. "We can set something up," the reply read. "John's team is always interested in Adobe's creative tools."

I kept the potential backstage access a secret when I told Jayson about the meeting. I wanted to manage our expectations.

Fast forward to the resort in Cancun. The air was thick with humidity and anticipation as we made our way through the winding paths of the all-inclusive resort. Palm trees swayed overhead, and the distant sound of waves crashing against the shore provided a constant backdrop to the excited chatter of concert-goers.

"So where exactly are we meeting these guys?" Jayson

asked, his Grateful Dead t-shirt damp with sweat in the Mexican heat.

"Near the production area," I said, trying to sound casual while my heart raced with anticipation. Would they come through with what they'd hinted at?

We turned a corner, and a serious-looking security guard stood beside a nondescript door. I gave our names, and his stern expression didn't change as he checked his list. Then, with a slight nod, he opened the door.

"Holy shit," Jayson whispered as we walked into the backstage area. Guitar techs were tuning instruments, crew members rushed around with purpose, and in the corner stood members of John Mayer's team waiting for us.

The meeting went well, and there was genuine interest in potential collaborations between Adobe and Mayer's creative projects. But the magical moment came at the end when they handed us four passes on lanyards.

"These will get you into the VIP section," the tour manager explained. "And if you want to return during the second set, you can watch from the side stage."

I'll never forget Jayson's look—part disbelief, part excitement, part gratitude. Later that night, as we stood mere feet from Mayer and the remaining members of the Grateful Dead, watching Shampa's face light up with each song, I realized something profound about relationship building.

The strongest connections aren't forged through big budgets or fancy dinners. They're created when you find ways to deliver experiences that touch something meaningful to the other person. Adobe had been a client for years at that point. Still, it was this moment—seeing their genuine joy as lifelong Deadheads watching their musical heroes from the side of the stage—that cemented a relationship that would withstand job changes, agency shifts, and all the everyday business challenges that typically end client relationships.

Anyone could have gone with them to Mexico. But the magic happened because I took the time to understand what truly mattered to them beyond business and found a way to make that happen.

If you bring that back to a more significant lesson regarding client experiences and how you wine and dine, anybody can outspend each other. You can get tickets to a concert, go to a fancy restaurant, or get terrific seats at the Super Bowl. There are certain things that, as long as you have enough money, are pay-to-play, and it'll work out for you as long as you have a big enough expense account. You can definitely provide that experience to your client.

But then there's this next level of experience that money can't buy. That's where you leverage your network and connections to provide access. For those backstage passes to the Grateful Dead show in Mexico, if you have a concierge or personal assistant, they could likely find the right person and pay enough money to get those, no matter what. Because we had the connections, that's something that we didn't have to pay for. Still, we enhanced their experience and made it more remarkable because we leveraged our industry connections, got to the right people, set up the right meetings, and elevated our experience even higher. That was something that I couldn't just go on StubHub and pay for that experience. I had to work my network.

When I interviewed the chief revenue officer of Twitch on my podcast, I asked him, "What do you guys do for client development? What conferences do you all go to?" He told me they don't go to any of the big conferences or trade shows. They focus 100% of their client development on providing experiences for clients they can't get on their own, whether that's access to a dinner with a chef from a TV show on Netflix or something similar. They're just constantly trying to figure out how to design these client experiences that are so elevated and are based on their connection as an Amazon holdings company, as well as the access that they have to celebrities. How can they create those elevated experiences?

It stuck with me that an organization as big as Twitch within the Amazon media network is exclusively focused on experiences regarding taking care of its clients and building relationships.

Jayson and I are honest, true friends at this point. From the outset, I was purposeful about going deep and relating to him personally in as many areas as possible to make that relationship as sticky as possible—not in a fake or manipulative way, not in a short-term way, and not in a shallow way, as if just focused on a single sale. That's the basic idea of *deep persuasion* and what *deep sales* means.

How do you go deep with a client? You start with the common ground, however small, and you cultivate it purposefully. You don't fake it; you don't force it. You find the intersection of personal and professional relevance and nurture that space. That's how you transform prospects into partners, customers into comrades, and contacts into lifelong friends. It's an approach to sales that requires patience, precision, and a lot of personal investment. But the payoff? It's not just measured in revenue but in relationships that last. While this deep relationship-building approach proved incredibly valuable with Jayson, it starkly contrasts with how most sales are conducted today. Traditional sales methods fail precisely because they prioritize volume over depth and quantity over quality.

When discussing "going deep" in business relationships,

I'm describing a specific approach that differs from traditional networking or sales relationship management. Going deep means intentionally developing relationships that transcend transactional interactions to create authentic human connections characterized by mutual trust, understanding, and value creation.

<u>At its core,</u> <u>going deep involves five key elements:</u>

- *Authentic connection*: Building relationships based on genuine curiosity and interest in the other person beyond their business utility.
- *Appropriate vulnerability*: Sharing and receiving personal insights that accelerate trust-building while maintaining professional boundaries.
- *Long-term orientation*: Focusing on the relationship's enduring value rather than immediate transaction potential.
- *Mutual value creation*: Consistently looking for ways to add value to the other person's life and business, even when there's no direct benefit to you.
- *Intentional depth*: Strategically investing more time and energy in relationships with the most potential for mutual growth.

Going deep doesn't mean treating every business contact like a best friend or spending endless hours on relationship maintenance. It means thoughtfully determining which relationships deserve deeper investment and strategically building those connections naturally and authentically for both parties. This is distinctly different from conventional business networking, which often emphasizes quantity over quality, immediate utility over long-term connection, and surface-level pleasantries over meaningful exchanges. The deep approach requires more initial investment, but creates increasingly valuable and self-sustaining relationships.

How do you accelerate relationships with your clients and prospects? How do you go deep, fast? And how do you turn those into meaningful relationships versus accounts or customers as fast as possible? It's about crafting relationships with a laser-focused strategy underpinned by authenticity. It's about identifying the right moment to reach out and doing so with a blend of personal touch and professional relevance. It's about the long game, playing it with the finesse of a chess grandmaster, thinking five moves ahead. You might wonder: 'How can I go deep with everyone? There aren't enough hours in the day.' You're right—and I'll address this challenge directly. Rather than attempting the impossible feat of forming deep relationships with everyone, I'll show you how to strategically identify which relationships deserve your most profound investment, warrant consistent attention, and can be maintained at scale through different approaches. The key isn't trying to defy human cognitive limitations—it's making intentional choices about where to invest your relationship energy for maximum mutual benefit.

Why traditional sales methods are failing

The old sales playbook is crumbling. I see it daily: seasoned sales professionals struggling because they're still using the same tactics that worked a decade ago. They're still focused on cold calls and elevator pitches, thinking of sales as a numbers game where more activity automatically equals more results. But here's the reality: the world has fundamentally changed.

Of course, there's the technology barrier. Sales used to be simple. You called, and they answered. Now, AI filters your emails, cell numbers are locked down, and the 'smile and dial' playbook is dead. Then there's the trust factor. We live in an age where people are bombarded with hundreds of sales messages daily. They've developed a sophisticated radar for detecting anything that feels like a sales pitch. Those carefully scripted cold calls and template emails? They're being deleted before they even get a chance. Traditional sales tactics have become so apparent that they're working against us.

Today's buyers don't need salespeople for information—they've already researched 80% of their decisions before you even enter the picture. They don't need someone to walk them through features and benefits. They need a trusted advisor who can add value beyond what they can find on Google. I see this playing out in the media and advertising world. In the past, media buyers would meet with sales reps because that was how they learned about new platforms and opportunities. Now? They can research everything themselves. The only reason to take a meeting is if they believe you will bring insights or opportunities they can't find anywhere else. That means having deep industry knowledge, genuine relationships, and the ability to connect dots in ways an internet search can't.

Look at what happened with traditional ad sales. The old model was based on relationships, but surface-level ones like taking media buyers to fancy dinners, entertaining them at sporting events, and becoming their "best friend" for the length of a contract. That worked when advertising was more straightforward and less data-driven. Now? Those same media buyers are being held accountable for every dollar they spend. They need partners who understand their business and can help them navigate complex ecosystems. A nice dinner does not cut it anymore. The companies that get this are completely rewriting their sales playbooks. They're moving away from high-pressure tactics and towards consultative relationships. They're investing in deep industry expertise. Most importantly, they recognize that genuine human connection becomes more valuable in a world where almost everything can be automated or digitized.

This shift occurs across every industry, not just in media and advertising. Traditional sales methods are failing because they were designed for a world that no longer exists. In the old world, information was scarce, buyers needed salespeople to learn about products, and relationships could be built on superficial interactions. That world is gone. The future belongs to those who can build genuine, value-driven relationships beyond transactional ones.

This isn't about wholly abandoning traditional sales skills–the fundamentals of understanding customer needs and communicating value will always matter. However, it is about recognizing that these skills must be applied differently. It's about moving from persuasion to partnership, moving from pitching to problem-solving, and building lasting relationships. Once you understand this shift and start focusing on building deep, authentic relationships rather than just hitting sales targets, everything else becomes more manageable. Your network starts working for you. Opportunities come to you. Most importantly, you build trust that no sales script or technique can replicate.

But if traditional high-pressure sales tactics no longer work, what does? Sometimes, the most powerful tool in modern sales makes most salespeople deeply uncomfortable: silence. My early understanding of relationship depth came from learning when to stop talking.

The art of silence

So many salespeople just don't know when to shut up.

Over the years, I've learned that sometimes, nothing at all is the most powerful thing you can say. It's about letting the space after a tricky question fill up with tension and potential, waiting for the prospect to break it. This is a strategy, not a fallback.

This opinion harkens back to my early days working in a boiler room. At that point in my career, I had a sales manager who, if he heard me on the phone just yapping away for too long with some prospect, and he felt like the person was just talking to me because he wanted to speak to me. He wasn't a buyer, and he wasn't going to buy; my boss would come out of his office, get right in my face, and feed me a power line like, "Hey, Bob, you know, you seem very interested in this. So, are you willing to commit to looking at this seriously today?" He would feed me some gnarly rip-the-Band-Aid-off-type qualifying questions to ask the person to see if they were just stroking me and wanting to talk because some people just enjoy talking when you get them on the phone. They'll have a conversation with you for an hour, even though they have no intention of actually buying your service or product.

When you can come at them with a hardcore qualifying question, stop and not say a word–it is uncomfortable, but I still do it. When I want to get down to qualifying questions like, "Do you guys have anything coming up that would potentially be a good fit for the solution?" Or "Do you guys have a timeline?" Or "Are you guys thinking about working with influencers, and what influencers?" I have a handful of power qualifiers to ask when I need to move things to the point. And when you are quiet and just shut up entirely and don't say a word, it creates discomfort. Being completely quiet and throwing it into your prospects' court is awkward. Sometimes, you have to start counting in your head literally: *one Mississippi, two Mississippi*. Just sitting there could be 10 seconds of long, torturous silence.

The power of silence in sales interactions cannot be overstated. When wielded skillfully, it can cut through the noise, create space for reflection, and compel prospects to confront their true intentions. A purposeful pause can profoundly impact a world constantly bombarded with information and chatter. It signifies confidence, invites introspection, and shifts the dynamic from a one-sided pitch to a two-way dialogue.

Mastering the art of silence requires practice and courage. It means being comfortable with discomfort, trusting in the strength of your offer, and having the patience to let the prospect come to you. It's not about manipulating or strong-arming, but rather it is about creating an environment where prospects can express their needs and commitment. When done right, strategic silence can be the catalyst that turns a meandering conversation into a decisive moment of clarity and action. So next time you find yourself in a sales conversation, remember–sometimes, the most influential thing you can say is nothing at all.

Silence in sales is not a new, sophisticated technique. Some of the old-school guys were absolute masters at it. Take Ray Kroc, who built McDonald's into what it is today. Despite his faults, he was great at negotiation. He had an incredible technique that would drive people crazy: He'd just sit there and say nothing after hearing an offer. I'm not talking about a few seconds here. This guy would sometimes go silent for whole minutes during negotiations.

There's this story about him in a real estate deal, who knows if it's true, but it's spoken of in sales lore. He's sitting across from this property owner who's trying to sell him a prime location for a new McDonald's. The seller throws out their price, and Kroc doesn't say anything. At all. The seller starts getting antsy, trying to fill the silence, explaining the value, and justifying the price—still nothing from Kroc. When he finally opened his mouth again, the seller had already dropped their price by 20% because they couldn't handle the silence.

This is precisely what I'm talking about when I say silence is power. It's not about being difficult or playing mind games. It's about giving people space to think about what they're saying and what they want. Sometimes, the best thing you can do is just shut up and let the other person work through their thoughts. Maybe it's best not to go as far as Kroc did, so you don't seem like a psycho for not responding to someone, but somewhere in between can be the difference between a good deal and a great deal. This strategic use of silence is just one example of how going deep requires us to reject conventional sales wisdom. Throughout my career, I've discovered that the most powerful sales tools are often counterintuitive.

TAKEAWAYS FROM CHAPTER 1:

- Prioritize relationship depth over transaction volume. Build authentic connections that

naturally lead to business growth rather than focusing solely on closing deals.
- Master strategic silence in sales conversations. Learn when to stop talking and let prospects fill uncomfortable gaps. When you listen instead of talking, you learn.
- Invest in relationships before you need them. The most valuable business relationships are built on genuine connection, not immediate need.
- Recognize why traditional sales methods fail. In today's world, buyers need trusted advisors who add value beyond what they can find online.

CHAPTER 2

The authenticity premium

I've noticed something interesting over the years: the deals that work out best aren't necessarily the ones that start with the most enormous budgets. They're the ones that begin with the most honest conversations about what's possible. Last year, I was working with a skincare brand that had just raised a significant round of funding. They came to us ready to spend big on influencer marketing. Most agencies would have been salivating over the budget, but something felt off. I realized they hadn't thought through their distribution strategy during our early conversations. They were ready to spend seven figures on influencer marketing, but their product wasn't consistently available in stores yet.

Instead of putting together a massive proposal, I suggested we start with a small test campaign focused on their strongest markets. This meant turning down a potentially substantial initial deal. But here's what happened: because we prioritized what would work over what would make us the most money, we built trust. That trust led to them bringing us in on their distribution strategy, which led to a much more effective overall campaign when we did scale up. This transparency is a perfect example of going deep in action—the authentic connection and long-term orientation elements we covered in Chapter 1. By prioritizing honest communication over short-term gain, you build the foundation for deeper trust.

However, this emphasis on authenticity and vulnerability has created an unexpected challenge: we're experiencing an epidemic of fake vulnerability, particularly in professional contexts. You see it everywhere, from social media to corporate culture—people sharing personal struggles or challenges in ways that feel calculated rather than genuine. Influencers craft vulnerable backstories designed primarily to boost engagement. Executives share rehearsed failures that inevitably highlight their resilience and insight. People are developing increasingly sophisticated radars for distinguishing between genuine vulnerability and performative openness. They're looking for the raw, unfiltered truth, not polished tales spun for likes, shares, or professional advancement.

Consider the contrast between two client relationships I experienced. I maintained a standard professional relationship with the first client, Mike: business-oriented conversations, regular lunches, campaign updates, and pleasant small talk. When a competitor offered slightly better rates, he left without hesitation. The relationship was replaceable because it never transcended transactions. With Jayson at Adobe, however, we gradually built something deeper. We shared resources, introduced our families, and supported each other through challenges. When competitors approached him with better offers, he didn't even consider them. The trust and connection we'd built went far beyond business terms.

The distinction is clear: shallow relationships are transactional, focused on what each person can extract from the other. Deep relationships are built on authentic connections, shared experiences, and mutual growth. They're not just about what you can get but about who you can become together.

<u>True vulnerability in business relationships means being willing to:</u>

- Admit when you don't know something.
- Acknowledge limitations in your product or service.
- Share appropriate professional challenges you've faced.
- Express genuine concern for the other person's success.
- Show up as a complete human being, not just a business function.

This kind of authentic vulnerability accelerates trust-building far more effectively than any sales technique. However, it must come from genuine openness rather than strategic manipulation. People can sense when vulnerability is weaponized as a sales tactic, and few things can damage trust more quickly than that. The authenticity premium in business is real and substantial—but it can only be earned through genuine openness, not performed vulnerability designed to create an effect. When you prioritize authentic connection over impression management, you build relationships that can withstand competitive pressures and create value far beyond the immediate transaction.

But isn't this still just manipulation?

When I discuss strategic relationship building, I often see skeptical looks. The question inevitably arises: "Isn't this just sophisticated manipulation? How can planning relationship development be authentic?"

It's a profound question that deserves serious consideration. The concern is legitimate—if we intentionally develop business relationships, are we merely instrumentalizing human connection for profit? Authenticity and strategy aren't mutually exclusive. I believe they must coexist for ethical, sustainable business practice. The difference between manipulation and strategic authenticity lies in three key areas: intention, transparency, and reciprocity.

Manipulation seeks to extract value through deception, creating an illusion of connection to achieve one-sided gain. Strategic authenticity, by contrast, aims to create mutual value through genuine understanding. I approach each relationship with the intention to understand the other person's goals, challenges, and perspectives—not to exploit them but to identify where authentic connection might create value for us both. This intention exists regardless of whether a business transaction ever materializes. Consider the relationship with Jayson at Adobe. My intention wasn't to "manipulate" him into buying more services. It was to understand his world deeply enough that I could genuinely help solve his challenges. The business results were a natural byproduct of that understanding, not its purpose.

Manipulation thrives on opacity—the manipulator conceals their true motives. Strategic authenticity, however, requires transparency about your professional context and goals. I'm always clear that I'm building relationships in a business context. I don't pretend our connection exists in a purely social vacuum—and interestingly, this honesty typically strengthens rather than weakens the relationship. Most professionals appreciate this clarity; they're building relationships for similar reasons.

This transparency extends to acknowledging the limitations of my expertise or solutions when they aren't the right fit. My willingness to say, "We're not the right partner for this particular need" has paradoxically led to deeper trust and often more business in areas where we truly excel. Perhaps the clearest distinction between manipulation and strategic authenticity is reciprocity. Manipulation creates an imbalanced value exchange, while strategic authenticity seeks mutual benefit and growth.

When I invest in understanding someone's business challenges, I'm not creating a debt they must repay with purchases. I'm initiating a reciprocal relationship where we both have opportunities to add value according to our unique capabilities and contexts. The test of this approach is straightforward: Would I still value and invest in this relationship even if I knew it would never lead to a direct business outcome? The answer is an unequivocal yes for many of the relationships I'll describe throughout this book. Some might argue that authentic connections should develop organically, without strategic consideration. This perspective holds an idealized view of authenticity that doesn't reflect how meaningful relationships form in any context—business or personal.

Think about dating. Planning thoughtfully for a first date—choosing the restaurant, considering conversation topics, reflecting on shared interests—doesn't make your interest fake. It shows you care enough to invest thought in the experience. Similarly, being intentional about professional relationships doesn't diminish their authenticity; it demonstrates respect for their value.

All lasting relationships require authentic connection and intentional cultivation. My approach simply makes explicit what successful relationship builders have always done intuitively. The most successful relationships are those where I genuinely care about the other person's success, independent of what they might do for me. This selfless orientation typically leads to better business outcomes than a transactional or selfish approach.

This isn't just idealism—it's practical. When you truly care about someone's success, you listen attentively, understand their needs more deeply, and ultimately create more value. This genuine care becomes the foundation for trust that can withstand the inevitable challenges of any business relationship. Maintaining this care is key even when immediate business returns aren't evident. If your attention to a relationship immediately disappears when a deal falls through, that reveals your true intentions were transactional all along. Rather than lowering our expectations for authenticity in business, I propose raising our standards for all professional interactions. We should expect business relationships to involve genuine human connection, mutual value, and long-term orientation.

The going deep approach isn't about manipulating people more effectively—it's about transforming how we understand business relationships entirely. It rejects the false choice between authentic connection and strategic purpose, recognizing that the most valuable relationships achieve both simultaneously. When we approach relationships with authentic interest in creating mutual value, we don't just do better business—we create a more humane and fulfilling professional environment for everyone involved.

The psychology of going deep

I'm no psychologist, but I've noticed something fascinating about deep business relationships—they tap into the same basic human needs as the rest of our relationships. There's this concept in psychology called "psychological safety." It's the idea that people need to feel safe being themselves, taking risks, and being vulnerable with others. When I first heard about this, it clicked immediately with my experiences. Take, once again, my favorite example of Jayson at Adobe. When we moved from formal business meetings to smoking cigars together and eventually to family vacations in Mexico, we gradually built psychological safety with each other. Each step allowed us to be more authentic and share more of ourselves.

Science backs this up in ways that might surprise you. Dr. Amy Cuddy from Harvard Business School studied first impressions for years and found something counterintuitive. In her research on how we evaluate people when we first meet them, she discovered that while we think competence matters most, warmth and trustworthiness make the most decisive impact. Her studies show that up to 82% of our evaluation of others comes down to two questions: "Can I trust this person?" and "Can I respect this person?"—with trust being the first filter we apply.

This isn't just theoretical. Neuroscience research from Dr. Paul Zak at Claremont Graduate University identified that when we feel trusted by someone, our brains produce oxytocin, often called the "trust hormone." This same neurochemical response is triggered during close personal bonds like parent-child relationships. His research shows that higher oxytocin levels correlate directly with increased willingness to engage in business transactions, explaining why relationship depth fundamentally changes buying behavior.

This explains why my approach to the John Mayer backstage experience worked so well. I wasn't just offering them an extraordinary experience—I was demonstrating trustworthiness by following through on something personally meaningful to them. The relationship had already established enough safety that I could learn what truly mattered to them (their love of the Grateful Dead), and they felt comfortable sharing that passion.

Think about the moments when your business relationships deepened. I bet they involved some appropriate vulnerability, like when I shared stories of my early boiler room days or when a client opened up about their challenges. These exchanges aren't just pleasantries; they're creating neurological connections that form the basis of trust.

Here's what I've learned about the psychology of deep relationships in business:

- *Trust is biological*: When we feel connected to someone, our brains release oxytocin—the same chemical that bonds parents to children. That's why face-to-face meetings are so powerful. You can't get that chemical response from an email. This explains why taking the time to fly to San Francisco for that first meeting with Jayson created such a strong foundation.

- *Reciprocity is automatic.* When someone shares something personal with us, we naturally want to share back in turn. But it has to be genuine. Like those performative social media posts, people can smell fake vulnerability a mile away.
- *Shared experiences create lasting bonds.* That's why I love getting out of the office with clients. Whether traveling to Cancun for concerts or weathering challenging business situations, these shared experiences fast-track relationship building.
- *We trust people who remind us of ourselves.* This isn't about superficial similarities. It's about finding genuine common ground in values, challenges, and aspirations. This is why I work to find authentic connection points, whether it's through Sigma Chi, a shared interest in cigars, or similar family situations.
- *Fear holds us back.* The most significant barrier to deep relationships isn't lack of opportunity, but fear. Fear of rejection, fear of looking unprofessional, fear of crossing boundaries. Despite our worries, the reward almost always outweighs the risk.

UNDERSTANDING these psychological principles is crucial, but they raise an obvious question: How do you maintain authentic connections as your network grows? Most people think you have to choose between depth and scale. That's a false choice, but it requires a different relationship-building approach than most networking experts teach.

. . .

<u>Takeaways from Chapter 2:</u>

- Create authentic connections through genuine common ground. Look beyond surface-level similarities to establish meaningful relationships.
- Practice appropriate professional vulnerability. Share challenges and insights that build trust while maintaining professional boundaries.
- Avoid performative openness. People can distinguish between genuine vulnerability and calculated attempts to appear authentic.
- Establish psychological safety in business relationships. Create environments where honest communication can flourish.

CHAPTER 3

The scale paradox

People often ask me how I maintain authentic relationships as my network grows. The answer isn't what they expect. I tell them, "I don't." You can't have deep, meaningful relationships with everyone, and pretending otherwise is precisely the fake authenticity I warned about earlier. I learned this lesson the hard way.

Early in my career at Channel Factory (a media agency specializing in the type of YouTube ads you click "skip" on), I tried to be everything to everyone. I had this massive spreadsheet of contacts, and I'd set reminders to reach out to each one regularly, send thoughtful notes, and remember their kids' names. It was exhausting, and worse—it wasn't real. I was going through the motions of relationship-building without actually building relationships.

The breakthrough came when I stopped trying to scale relationships and instead focused on being genuinely present in each interaction. Some conversations will stay at the surface level, and that's okay. Others will naturally deepen over time. You can't force depth any more than you can move a friendship.

This tension between depth and scale isn't just something I've observed—it's a well-documented challenge in relationship science. Robin Dunbar extensively researched the cognitive limits on our social relationships. Dunbar's research reveals inherent brain limitations on the number of meaningful relationships we can sustain. So, here's how I resolve this paradox:

First, I categorize my relationships using a simple A, B, and C system:

- A-level connections are my key clients, super-connectors, and closest professional relationships—people like Jayson at Adobe. These are the relationships I invest most deeply in, where we might vacation together and where our families know each other. I have maybe 15-20 of these.
- B-level connections are past clients, active prospects, and people I genuinely like and respect professionally. We might meet quarterly for coffee or catch up at conferences. This circle includes about 100-150 people.
- The rest of my network consists of C—level connections—thousands of people I've met professionally with whom I want to stay connected but don't have the capacity for regular one-on-one interaction.

S<small>ECOND</small>, <u>I create appropriate engagement strategies for each level:</u>

- I focus on in-person experiences, deep conversations, and regular, meaningful touchpoints for A-level relationships. I might text Jayson about a great cigar I tried or plan trips together. It's a genuine friendship that happens to include business.
- I use a mix of personal outreach and group settings for B-level connections. I'll send them relevant articles, invite them to events I'm hosting, or meet one-on-one when I'm in their city. The key is making each interaction authentic, even if they're less frequent.
- I leverage content creation, my podcast, and occasional mass communications for C-level contacts that still carry my authentic voice. My newsletter goes to thousands, but I write it as if I'm talking directly to one person.

W<small>HEN</small> I <small>TRACKED</small> how I spent my time at Channel Factory, I discovered I invested 70% of my energy in shallow relationships that generated only 30% of my revenue. Meanwhile, the deep relationships I built produced 70% of my results with only 30% of my time investment. The resolution to the scale paradox isn't finding some magical way to have deep relationships with everyone—it's being intentional about where you invest your relationship energy. Deep relationships naturally create compound returns over time. My relationship with Jayson has generated millions in revenue over eight years, far more than dozens of transactional connections could produce.

This approach also creates a natural progression path. Some C-level connections will show the potential to become B-level connections, and some B-level connections will naturally evolve into A-level relationships. The paradox resolves when you stop seeing relationship-building as a volume game and start seeing it as an investment portfolio. You wouldn't put the same amount of money into every stock—you'd allocate strategically based on potential returns. Your relationship capital works the same way. Technology helps manage the logistics of relationship maintenance at scale, but it doesn't replace the human touch that makes those relationships meaningful. The question isn't whether depth scales—it's about applying the appropriate level of depth to different relationships based on their strategic importance and potential.

The unspoken contract

Here's something they don't teach you in sales training: every business relationship has an unspoken contract that's more important than the written one. It's about understanding what success looks like for everyone involved. I recently had a situation with a tech startup where the founder focused solely on metrics: engagement rates, click-throughs, and all the usual KPIs. In one of our casual conversations, he mentioned that he had trouble recruiting because his company wasn't seen as a cultural leader in their space. This wasn't in our brief or contract, but it became a key part of how we approached their influencer strategy.

We ended up creating content that not only drove

customer engagement but also helped position them as an innovative place to work. Their recruitment costs dropped significantly–a benefit we never initially discussed but that came from understanding what they needed beyond the metrics. Good business relationships aren't about avoiding tension–they're about using tension productively. I'm not talking about creating conflict but about leaning into the natural tension between two parties trying to achieve something meaningful together.

We've gotten good at tracking metrics and signals in the data analytics and AI age. But I've found that the most critical signals often don't appear in any dashboard. I was tracking all the usual engagement metrics for a significant campaign when I noticed something interesting: one of our client's junior team members was consistently sharing our content on their personal LinkedIn. Not because they had to, but because they genuinely found it valuable. This wasn't a KPI we were tracking, but it told me something important about how our work resonated within their organization. This led me to develop the "inside-out" theory of campaign success: if we can get the client's team excited about our work, external success usually follows. Now, I pay as much attention to how our work resonates internally with clients as I do to external metrics.

I've also learned to look at how a potential client treats their existing partners. I was once in a pitch where the prospect spent the first twenty minutes complaining about their current agency. They had a giant budget and seemed ready to sign with us, but those complaints were a red flag. Why would we be any different if they hadn't built a good relationship with their current partner? I had a frank discussion with them about what went wrong in their previous agency relationship and what they'd learned from it. This conversation helped change the dynamic. Instead of me just pitching my firm's capabilities, we talked about how to build a long-term partnership. They appreciated the honesty, which led to a much stronger foundation for our work together.

But what about time?

"This all sounds great, Dylan, but who has the time?" I hear this objection constantly, and it's valid. We're all juggling packed schedules, multiple priorities, and the pressure to deliver immediate results. Building deep relationships seems like a luxury when quarterly targets breathe down your neck.

But here's the counterintuitive truth I've discovered: going deep actually saves time in the long run. Think about how much time you spend chasing new prospects because your existing relationships aren't yielding enough business. Or how many hours you waste repairing misunderstandings that stemmed from shallow communication. Or the endless cycle of onboarding new clients because your retention isn't strong enough.

The real time-killer isn't depth—it's breadth without strategy. When trying to be everything to everyone, you end up being nothing significant to anyone. That's the actual time drain. Of course, there's a delicate balance here. We'll go into this more in-depth later, but I've sometimes gone too far with client relationships, flying across the country at a moment's notice and missing necessary family time. COVID-19 helped me recalibrate this balance. The key is being intentional about all of your relationships, including those with your family. The deep approach is ultimately about quality time rather than quantity, both with clients and with loved ones. When you apply the same thoughtfulness to your personal relationships that you do to your professional ones, you create a more sustainable approach to both.

Let me be clear: going deep initially requires more time and investment than traditional transactional approaches. The time savings come not from less time spent overall but from more efficient and effective use of that time. When I say it 'saves time in the long run,' I mean you'll spend less time chasing new business, repairing misunderstandings, and starting from zero with each prospect. Instead, you'll invest time more meaningfully in relationships that compound in value over the years.

Think of it as the difference between renting and owning a home. Renting (transactional relationships) might seem more manageable in the short term—less maintenance and less commitment. However, owning (deep relationships), while requiring more upfront investment and ongoing care, builds equity over time. Eventually, that equity will work for you in ways that renting never could. The time investment shifts from constant hunting to strategic nurturing, creating more space for professional success and personal fulfillment.

TAKEAWAYS FROM CHAPTER 3:

- Implement the A/B/C relationship framework to manage your network strategically at different depths.
- Recognize that you can't maintain deep relationships with everyone - Be intentional about where you invest your relationship energy.

- Understand the "unspoken contract" in business relationships. Look beyond formal agreements to what truly defines success for each party.
- Remember that going deep saves time in the long run. Deep relationships require less maintenance while producing more value.

PART II
THE STRATEGY

4

CHAPTER 4

Hunting with an elephant gun and a sniper rifle

You might notice a seeming contradiction in what follows: I'll present structured frameworks and specific approaches while simultaneously advocating for authentic, organic relationship development. Let me address this directly. The frameworks I offer aren't rigid formulas that replace genuine human connection—they're scaffolding that supports it. Just as learning proper technique helps musicians express themselves more authentically, these approaches provide a structure that enables more natural relationship building. They allow you to organize your thinking and actions to be more present and responsive in interactions.

Think of these frameworks as training wheels—necessary when developing new skills but eventually fading into the background as the principles become integrated into how you naturally operate. The goal isn't mechanical application of techniques but internalizing principles that enhance your authentic relationship-building style."

Early in my career, I was working in a boiler room, calling 100 attorneys a day to get them to invest in a film we were producing about a famous court case. My sales manager, Greg Cozine, saw something in me: that I had the talent to be a great salesperson, and that he saw my work ethic. You can't just be good. You have to have good raw talent, and you have to be moldable and teachable. But you also have to have a work ethic. So I'd show up early. Our hours were from 7 am to 1 pm, and most guys would pull the parachute (as Greg liked to say) right when we could leave the office; they would grab their stuff and take off. But I would stick around and continue to make calls, and then Greg would usually call me into his office, and we would just shoot the shit and talk about strategy, and talk about sales and talk about life. Greg would pull the parachute at 3 p.m., and I sometimes stayed until 9 p.m. I would call Hawaii. If I had more time, dials, reps, and chances, I would get better than all the other guys. I was able to make a living at a time when many people in 2008 were hiding their money under a mattress, much less investing in a movie. But that was a relationship where Greg added a lot of value to my life, and I learned a lot from my time working for him.

Last year, we targeted the consumer packaged goods (CPG) sector for our influencer marketing services. Every Monday morning, I'd start with my elephant gun approach: sending personalized but templated outreach to 200+ marketing directors and VPs in the CPG space using our CRM. These messages highlighted recent case studies, industry trends, and a clear call to action. This broad outreach consistently generated a handful of weekly responses—maybe 5-8 people expressing some interest. That's where the sniper rifle came in. I'd switch to deep research mode for each of those initial responses. Before following up, I'd spend 30-45 minutes per prospect learning everything I could about them. I'd read their LinkedIn posts and comments going back months. I'd find interviews they'd given. I'd look up their previous companies and roles. I'd identify mutual connections and ask those people for insights about the prospect's working style and priorities.

One particular CPG marketing director responded with mild interest to my elephant gun outreach: "This might be relevant for us later this year. Feel free to check back in Q2." Most salespeople would set a calendar reminder and move on. Instead, I noticed from her LinkedIn activity that she was passionate about sustainable packaging. I also discovered through a mutual connection that her team had recently faced criticism for a campaign that underperformed with Gen Z audiences. My follow-up wasn't a generic "checking in" message. I sent her an in-depth article about sustainable packaging innovations that might interest her, specifically in her product category. I mentioned nothing about our services. She responded enthusiastically, and we had a 15-minute call. At the end of that call, I briefly mentioned a case study we had about reaching Gen Z authentically. That led to a proper meeting where we discussed her team's challenges in detail.

The elephant gun got me initial awareness and a basic response. The sniper rifle turned that basic response into a meaningful relationship based on providing specific value aligned with her actual priorities, not just our sales goals. Here's another example of these approaches working in tandem. During COVID-19, I needed to adapt my relationship-building strategy when in-person events disappeared. My elephant gun approach became a weekly LinkedIn newsletter where I shared influencer marketing trends with my entire network. This broad-reaching content kept me visible to thousands of connections with minimal time investment on my part. The sniper rifle element came in how I used engagement with that content. When someone I hadn't connected with in years commented on a newsletter post, I immediately switched to personalized outreach: "John, great to see your thoughts on my recent post. I noticed you've moved to XYZ company. How are you doing with the transition? I recently worked with a brand in your space that faced [specific challenge]. Happy to share what we learned if that's something your team is navigating too."

This combined approach led to a meeting with a former colleague who had moved to a major beverage brand. What started with broad content (elephant gun) and followed with specific, personalized outreach (sniper rifle) resulted in an account that's still with us today. The key to making these approaches work together is timing and an authentic transition. The elephant gun creates initial awareness and a basic connection, permitting you to engage. The sniper rifle then deepens that connection through specific, relevant value, but it only works because the initial groundwork is already laid. Without the elephant gun's broad reach, you'd have too few opportunities to deploy your sniper rifle effectively. Without the sniper rifle's precision and personalization, your elephant gun connections would remain shallow.

Most importantly, this dual approach system becomes more effective over time. As your sniper rifle builds deeper relationships, those relationships generate referrals and introductions, creating targeted opportunities that bypass the need for elephant gun outreach. Eventually, the balance shifts from mostly elephant gun to sniper rifle, but you never abandon either approach entirely.

The strategic balance between broad outreach and targeted connection I'm advocating isn't just my approach—

it's supported by network theory research. Dr. Brian Uzzi of Northwestern University studied over 20,000 business relationships and identified what he calls "the paradox of embeddedness." His research revealed that the most successful professionals maintain what he terms a "dual network structure"—a combination of strong, deep ties (what I call the sniper rifle approach) and a broader network of weaker connections (the elephant gun approach). Those with this balanced network structure consistently outperformed those focused exclusively on deep or broad connections. His research showed a 31% higher revenue generation for professionals who maintained this dual structure than those who didn't.

Most sales gurus and coaches tend to be one or the other. I suggest that you do both. You must get your elephant gun reps out early in the day and spend the rest of your time on the sniper rifle. Ensure you get both the numbers in as well as the more personalized, direct outreach, custom-tailored to the person. In my example of meeting Jayson at Adobe, LinkedIn is great. It gives you different signals based on what's happening inside your network, whether people are sharing things or moving to new roles and companies. As I mentioned in the opening pages, one of my favorite signals is when people change positions and move to a new job. When somebody moves to a new job, one of two things happens. They hit the ground running at a company, and they're at a fast-paced job where they end up with a clean slate, an empty inbox, and no preexisting relationships other than the ones they inherited. That's a great time to touch base with people. LinkedIn signals allow you to reach out and touch base with your network.

Dale Carnegie famously said, "You can make more

friends in two months by becoming interested in other people than you can in two years by trying to get other people interested in you." This quote underscores the essence of persuasion—it's not about manipulating others to do what you want but about genuinely engaging with them, understanding their needs, and working together toward a shared goal.

Studies have shown that sales professionals who prioritize relationship-building over aggressive selling techniques achieve higher customer retention rates. For instance, a Salesforce study revealed that customers who feel their salesperson is looking out for their best interests are more likely to consider purchasing from that person again.

Thus, the art of persuasion is not just about how much pressure you can exert or how many calls you can make in a single day. Going deep is about the depth of the relationships you cultivate. When we approach each interaction with the intent to understand and add value to each other, we do not just sell; we build trust. In the end, the "success" of our relationships will be measured not by the quantity of transactions we've completed but by the quality of the relationships we've nurtured. This is the essence of deep persuasion, where each connection we make enriches our professional journey and, more importantly, our lives. It's not just about choosing the right tactics. Your network becomes a force multiplier when you approach it correctly.

This dual approach directly supports the going deep framework. The elephant gun creates initial contacts at scale, while the sniper rifle allows you to move selected relationships into deeper context and connection rings. It's about creating a pipeline of relationships that can be developed at varying depths based on mutual interest and potential.

Practice what you preach

When creating content, I document it because it's relevant to my professional life and gives my network a glimpse into my why. If they help Dylan, they're helping his family. I make thoughtful comments when I go through my LinkedIn feed and come across interesting posts. I recently posted about bringing cigars to an event, and through the comments, I planned a networking event with someone I'd only met once. I try to be funny in my comments without being snarky or condescending. For example, when Manscaped announced a partnership with Best Buy, I jokingly commented, "Are they going to do in-store demos?" The SVP of Manscaped loved it and called it the best comment of the week, and we started chatting about meeting up. I tag solutions and companies even when I don't work for them.

You have to invest in your marketing. If you're a Wall Street stockbroker or financial advisor, you master how financial markets work. You invest other people's money, but you also invest your own money and make your money from Wall Street. Real estate agents buy and sell real estate; it's how they make and invest their money. Most purchase real estate properties and put them on Airbnb, using their practical knowledge of the real estate market to grow their wealth. But then, when you look at people like me who are in advertising and marketing, many of us don't take our savings or extra cash and invest that back into marketing ourselves. We invest in the traditional things that are supposed to build wealth, such as crypto, real estate, or the stock market. The number one thing that you could invest in as a marketer is marketing. The absolute number one place you could have the most likely outcome of a return on investment is by investing in the marketing channels you know how to run. If you are good at SEM, invest in SEM. If you're good at influencer marketing, invest in influencer marketing. If you are good at content marketing, invest dollars into content marketing to promote yourself, your brand, and your company.

Many people probably say, "I don't have anything to market, I don't have a company, and I don't have a business." There are many different ways to get started, such as quickly creating a monetization strategy for your marketing. If you want to become an affiliate of any company you like, and you can figure out a way to generate an acquisition that is lower than the cost of what they pay as an affiliate, then you could do marketing. You don't have to go and spin up a company or start a brand. You can be an affiliate for a brand already out there that you trust or admire, and you can just do marketing to get acquisitions and make a profit margin.

The most significant single transfer of wealth in American history is with baby boomers entering retirement age. Businesses are going up for sale every single day. Baby boomers are entering retirement and won't just hand over those businesses to their kids. You can go on websites like BizBuySell and look for all these types of businesses: mom-and-pop style operations, service businesses, consumer products businesses, retail businesses, and many others. These are companies that have only invested a little in marketing. Many of these folks just want out because they're of retirement age. You can acquire these businesses for pennies on the dollar. You can negotiate favorable terms and apply your marketing expertise to increase profitability, cash flow, and the top line. We usually think about starting a business, but the reality is that 90% of startups end up failing. Why not go out there and find a business that's already successful and acquire it instead? Then, apply your marketing skills to that business.

You can join the freelance economy. Join the gig economy as a consultant. Market yourself to other potential clients and agencies as a fractional worker. So many marketers are great at doing marketing for clients, but when it comes to marketing themselves, they could be better at it. We do the best work for our clients, so we need more time to do it ourselves. We're entering an age where authenticity is essential for businesses, too. Do I use my service to generate results for myself? I want to see them prove that they do whatever they do as a marketer and use that same capability or process to develop their business. If you can't do what you tell me you can do for yourself, why should I trust you to do it for me or my clients? Marketers must apply the superpowers they've learned to their business models and invest extra cash into building their businesses and personal brands. When you run a campaign yourself, you're much more diligent in tracking it and seeing the outcome. I've checked a hundred-dollar Snapchat ad that I ran for my podcast more times than a $500,000 campaign for a client. You're much more in the weeds when it's your money. You want it to perform. You're a lot more diligent in ensuring it generates the intended result. Marketers need to invest in themselves.

One of the most complex parts of professional services is that they are not generally products that can be sold through e-commerce or unaided sales. An unaided sale is when a user can come to your website, find all the information they need, research you, swipe their credit card, and be done with it. All you have to do is get them to your website. An unaided sale is really what you want to shoot for because it doesn't require a salesperson.

In service industries, this has always been hard. You would have to drive people to your website, but then you would have to get them to either book a meeting or email you to find more information. Give your email address to be marketed to in exchange for value. Most service providers are so convoluted that they think they can't just offer something for purchase on their website—options for $1,000, $2,000, or $3,000 packages, for instance. In the services industry, create an easy, frictionless e-commerce experience in the sales process to qualify customers and determine the opportunity.

If we were intelligent marketers, we would think about user experience. We would think about how people are used to buying things online that they've never purchased online before. You wouldn't have been able to buy a car through a website like Carvana or Vroom just a few years ago. I've sold two cars and purchased three through these online sites for tens of thousands of dollars. I didn't care that I couldn't talk to a salesperson or see the car before buying it. I went to those sites specifically to avoid an antiquated sales process. I didn't want to deal with a salesperson. The same unaided sales process can work for professional services. You can provide a one-hour introductory consultation or a marketing strategy.

You can create sales funnels and drive traffic to your website, where your consumers can research, since you're putting out excellent information. They found you either through search or social. They are coming to you with a familiarity with what you do, who you are, your brand, and trust. They're willing to take out their credit card and spend money without ever talking to you. You can implement chatbots to help nudge them along the way. That chatbot will learn recurring questions and become more innovative through AI. You're going to get some customers who are old school and will only purchase a service from a professional if they get to know them first. The significant part about social media is that you can put out your best content, tips, and strategies for free across all channels. Then, when people come to your website, they're already familiar with you. They know you because you've already put out so much content. I use social selling, which means being active on social media and posting content aligned with your brand that lets people know what you're doing. But you can't just be a one-way distribution channel–you can't only post and not engage. Nobody will engage with you if you're not engaging with anybody, and no one will care that you're creating content.

I document my journey as a business development professional in the media industry. I get to do interesting things and meet people that the average person doesn't always get to do. I also interweave content about my family and traveling because that's relevant to my brand around my travel client, Lost In. I want people to see who I am professionally, my advice about being a good salesperson or marketer, and what drives me. I work to make money to support my family and take them on vacations. It's important to show people that dimension. Let's not just be greedy people making money to make money. Let's show people what we care about and where we spend our money.

Takeaways from Chapter 4:

- Balance "elephant gun" (broad outreach) with "sniper rifle" (targeted connection) approaches in your business development.

- Use content creation to scale relationship-building beyond what's possible through one-to-one interactions.
- Practice what you preach. Use your marketing expertise to build your personal brand and demonstrate your capabilities.
- Create opportunities for strategic connections through intentional presence in the right environments.

CHAPTER 5

Content as connection

When looking at tickets for conferences, I always look for press credentials. I don't reach out and say, "Hey, I'm the sales guy, and I want to sponsor. I want to buy the salesperson ticket," which most salespeople have to do. Usually, the salesperson's ticket is a lot more expensive. There is a direct-to-consumer conference the day before SXSW in Austin that the Founders Group organizes. If you're a brand, you get to attend for free, but if you're a vendor or a salesperson, you have to pay $2,500 to go. That's a big chunk. But they also have a press certification. If you're a member of the press or a member of the media, then you can get a free badge. So last year, I contacted these shows and said, "Hey, I'm a podcaster. Do you have a podcasting row? Would you like me to interview guests and sponsors?" I've gotten credentialed as an influencer or press for as many shows as I would have had to pay as a salesperson as a sponsor.

This strategy has become one of my most effective tools

for going deep with prospects quickly. It's not that every sales team needs a podcast, but for me, it's been transformative in creating genuine connections that traditional sales approaches simply can't match. I started my podcast in 2017. When I began to do the podcast, my idea was to interview Chief Revenue Officers. I wanted to interview the best and the brightest CROs at big media companies, social networks, ad tech companies, and publishers, and learn from the best of them so I could know what they do well. Then, I could get mentored by them for an hour at a time. My value proposition is to platform them with my 29,000 LinkedIn followers and the 40,000 people who subscribe to our newsletter.

What I discovered was something more potent than just learning—I was creating a context for relationship building that completely bypassed the traditional sales barriers. The podcast became a laboratory for going deep. My first episode was with Jonathan Simpson-Bint, Twitch's chief revenue officer. It was a great show, but then I started wanting to interview people I might do business with, like CMOs, instead of interviewing CROs. Usually, CMOs don't take meetings with sales guys unless you're a more significant, well-known commodity or platform. Surprisingly, even big CMOs will come on a podcast with very few questions asked.

This is where the magic happens—the same CMO who might ignore a traditional sales outreach will happily spend 45 minutes with me on a podcast. They're not interested in being sold to, but because the format creates mutual value, they get exposure, and I get relationship-building time that otherwise would be impossible to secure. What makes this approach effective is asking questions that naturally elicit more profound, more personal responses than in a traditional sales meeting.

Based on my experiences hosting the podcast, here are the types of questions I've found valuable for creating real depth:

- Questions about personal journeys rather than professional achievements: "I'd love to hear about your path to your current role. What parts of that story might surprise people who only know your professional side?"
- Questions that invite appropriate vulnerability: "What business challenge have you faced that taught you something important about yourself?"
- Questions that explore unique perspectives: "What's a principle you follow in your approach that might go against conventional wisdom in your industry?"
- Questions about formative experiences: "Was there a pivotal moment or decision that significantly shaped your leadership approach?"
- Questions about influences and inspiration: "Who or what has had the biggest impact on how you approach your work?"
- Questions that transition naturally to business topics: "How does your company currently think about [relevant areas to my business]? What's working well, and what are you still figuring out?"

The research process is a form of going deep before you've met the person. By immersing yourself in their world—their thinking, history, and perspectives—you're developing genuine curiosity and understanding that translates into a real connection during the conversation. A good sales manager will tell you that you should do your homework if you have a sales call or a business presentation. Research that person ahead of time and come up with interesting questions. Most salespeople show up to a sales presentation completely cold and use that call as an opportunity to make discoveries and get to know somebody. We should all do our homework before attending those calls and doing a podcast. You can't show up uninformed, or the show will suck.

The podcast format has been transformative, but the underlying principle is what matters: creating contexts where deeper, more authentic conversations can happen. Some sales professionals might find this through hosting events, writing a newsletter, or making other types of content. The specific format isn't what matters—it's about creating space for genuine connection beyond the typical sales interaction. My favorite part about the podcasting process is the research. I do all my research. I don't have a research assistant who writes my questions. I am doing my homework and absorbing the entire canon of information about a guest online, reading their books and listening to their audiobooks. It allows you to come up with fascinating, well-thought-out questions.

The podcast allows me to ask them any questions that I want to know about. I steer the conversation. I ask them about their career and personal questions about their life, and things I learned from doing the research on them that are interesting. I start building personal relationships and rapport, getting to know their business philosophy, marketing philosophy, and how they've built their careers. At the end of the podcast, I'll dovetail into questions that are leading questions, qualifying whether they're a good fit for me to do business with. I'll ask them about their influencer marketing programs, and I'll ask them what they think about LinkedIn as an influencer marketing platform. As they start to answer those questions, they'll either qualify themselves that they're not a good fit because they're not super focused on what I do, or they'll start to realize that they've got some gaps and some deficits in their knowledge and that I could be an excellent person to shore up some of those issues.

This natural progression from personal to professional creates the conditions for going deep in an organic way. There's no awkward transition from relationship building to business discussion—it flows naturally as part of the broader conversation about their work and challenges.

Instead of me doing a sales call that's behind closed walls with me and that prospect being the only beneficiaries, now that's broadcast to the entire world. I get between 4,000 and 5,000 views on each LinkedIn post. That's a decent audience getting exposed to my brand and the guests' brands while listening to our joint thought leadership. As I type this, my videos have probably been viewed by about 6,000 people through LinkedIn this week. As good as I am at doing outreach, getting a lot of touchpoints out there, and talking to many people each week, there's no way, physically, through technology, or otherwise, I could ever touch base with 6,000 people a week. It's only Wednesday. I still have a couple more days and could get to 10,000 views this week.

This is where content creation intersects with the dual approach I described earlier—the "elephant gun and sniper rifle" method. The podcast serves as my elephant gun, creating broad awareness and connection opportunities at scale, while the individual relationships I develop with guests represent the sniper rifle approach. That's different from an audience I could ever reach, being a one-to-one salesperson or even a one-to-many salesperson doing more programmatic outreach with AI and software. For me, podcasting has been a revelation, but the principle can work across different formats. If you're considering a similar approach, consider what format aligns with your strengths, industry, and the relationships you want to build. While podcasting works for me, others might find video series, written interviews, or community events more effective for their context.

If podcasting does interest you, the whole sales team can reach out and book guests, which gives everybody on the team an extra arrow in their quiver. Whoever's going to be the host gets an opportunity to shine. I'm a big fan of podcasting. Everybody's an influencer, and everybody can be a content creator, too. Some good podcasters just show up and hit the button, and the show is what it is, but my confidence level would be low if I hadn't done the research and come up with at least ten questions unique to that particular guest.

A podcast allows you to learn out loud. You're getting access to these extraordinary thought leaders. The podcast becomes your classroom, where you get to absorb all these cool concepts around marketing or advertising, or whatever the theme of your podcast is. You get to be the laboratory and the student because you're asking the questions.

Gary Vaynerchuk was someone who understood this concept before most people did. He started out running his family's wine shop in New Jersey. In 2006, when YouTube was still a baby, he launched a show called Wine Library TV. Just him, tasting wines, talking about them like a regular person instead of some stuffy wine snob. Gary wasn't just throwing content out there and hoping something would stick. He was doing exactly what I've been talking about with going deep. He responded to every single comment. Every email. Every person who reached out. He wasn't just creating content but was building relationships through that content.

Think about that for a second. This guy runs a wine shop in New Jersey, but he uses video content to build genuine connections with people worldwide. Many of these viewers became customers, and some even became business partners in his later ventures. This isn't just about putting stuff out there—it's about using content as a gateway to build actual relationships. The format isn't what matters—it's the intention behind it. Whether you choose podcasting, video, writing, or something else, the key is creating contexts to go beyond surface-level interactions and build fundamental understanding and trust. That's the essence of going deep.

Every salesperson needs to become a content creator

Salespeople, like anyone else, have a limited capacity. Our capacity is based on the scalability of how many meetings we can take on as individuals. If all business development people want to progress past being good salespeople, they must shift to being content creators. Not just creating content but also learning how to leverage paid media to get our voices out there in front of not hundreds of people but thousands of people.

Sabri Suby, the CEO of one of the fastest-growing agencies in Australia, called King Kong, and the author of a book called *Sell Like Crazy*, knows how to do this. The way I found out about him and his book is tied directly to how effective his strategy is: I saw a YouTube ad of his, and I decided to keep watching instead of clicking "skip." It was one of those typical, long YouTube videos of a guy doing a funny Dollar Shave Club-style advertisement, but then he goes on about sales and how to grow your pipeline. Then, he said if you click through and pay for shipping, he'll send you his book for free--so I did that and started reading it. I expected a lot of trash and fluff, a typical marketing piece where he wouldn't give away any good insights. I expected a bunch of hype to get readers further down his funnel, but as I continued to read past the first 70 pages, I found that it was way better than I expected.

Sabri's pathway as an agency leader didn't come from being a marketing guy. It came from being a sales guy. He started off selling and moved from Australia to London and took shitty door-to-door style sales jobs, and then eventually worked his way up into more complex SaaS-based sales products. He figured out that his capacity to earn or impact an organization was limited by how many meetings he could have every week and how many calls he could jump on. Even if you burn the candle at both ends, you can only have meetings between regular business hours. If you stack the deck, maybe you could do 5 to 6 calls or meetings per day at the most, so instead of selling one-to-one, he began selling one-to-many by creating videos that would go through whatever his value prop or his sales pitch was, and then he would not only rely on organic social for those videos to go out and find an audience, but he put paid media behind them, and that's when he started to scale his organization. That paid media strategy is how I discovered him through a YouTube ad and got his book. He gave away good advice in his video that was running as an ad to reach as many people as possible, then ended that video with a call to action to get a free copy of his book, in which he gave away better advice. And now, here I am talking about a success story to praise this guy I've never even spoken to.

Here's another example of this in action: I was doing research for a guest I had on my podcast named Jake Carl. Jake is only 30 and the CEO of one of Canada's fastest-growing, better-for-you healthy chocolate companies called Mid-day Squares. They're a healthy version of a chocolate bar mixed with a protein bar. What was exciting about researching this guy's marketing was that he has lived and breathed this concept he termed "Build Out Loud." He launched Mid-Day Squares after having two other semi-successful startups, one in the fitness space and one in the fashion space; he launched Mid-Day Squares with his sister and his sister's husband with the philosophy of broadcasting their entire journey.

Jake saw in the marketplace that, as a social media practitioner, there was an exciting triangle between Elon Musk, the Kardashians, and Shark Tank. If you think of someone like Elon Musk or the Kardashians, love or hate them, they've been successful because they've documented their entire lives, and people care to follow the intricacies. You combine that with the Shark Tank obsession–the public's interest in entrepreneurship.

When Jake joined his sister and brother-in-law to launch Mid-day Squares, his requirement from day one was what he referred to as building the company out loud. They would document every single part of the business journey. They intended to essentially air a 24-hour reality show of themselves as entrepreneurs and founders on social media.

It started with them setting up their iPhones and pressing record during meetings. Instead of building customers, they acquired fans, and the fans became not just people who liked their product, but because they had gotten to know them through social media, they weren't just buying these healthy snacks from a company. They bought them from friends because they had gotten to know and relate to them. They had given them the good, the bad, and the ugly of their story as they built this company.

Jake then made his first hire outside the core founders. It was a videographer. They found this strategy so necessary that the fourth employee at the company was a videographer. I'm not saying every founder needs to document every moment of their life, but people buy things from people, not companies. The more you show the world the real you via personal and professional social media, the more they will like you and want to do business with you. We don't all have to emulate the Kardashians or Elon Musk in every way, but there are numerous benefits to documenting your processes and sharing them as a branding exercise.

If you're going to live this process as an entrepreneur, documenting your journey, you should be thinking about how you invest and scale, and up-level your content. That should be one of the first things you focus on as an entrepreneur: How do you tell your story better? By documenting your process, you can create a feedback loop and get insight into what to pivot and correct in the course. You've got this opportunity to get out there and find audiences naturally through vertical videos like TikTok, Instagram Reels, and YouTube Shorts. They're just giving away free audiences if you can create engaging content.

Jake also got out there and started doing any speaking engagements he could. He didn't care what it was. If they invited him to go and talk to a college campus or an industry entirely irrelevant to food, he would accept any speaking opportunity possible. He treated his company's marketing as if it were a political campaign. He was on tour doing stumps, going from city to city. When you can speak in person and engage a crowd, you can inspire people and get them to buy into your journey. His whole process is, in turn, creating fans and friends, not just creating customers. Then, returning to Sabri's stuff, consider how his mindset relates to sales.

This concept that every salesperson needs to become a content creator can be incorporated in whatever way is most authentic to you, so as not to feel forced. I know a lot of salespeople who hear this advice and will go kicking and screaming because they didn't get into sales to be content marketers. They didn't get into sales because they wanted to be influencers or build a personal brand. They just wanted to smile and dial. I was that same way for a long time. I always wanted to outwork the competition by putting in more reps and hours. Thinking about the elephant gun approach of the numbers game aspects of sales, how many and how fast can you gather leads? How fast can you write a customized, relevant outreach email that adds value to a potential new prospect?

A salesperson has a point of limited, diminishing returns of how much outreach you can do each day. How many folks can you convert into a meeting and have a meaningful conversation with? This idea of building out loud is incredibly relevant to salespeople. You have to put yourself in the mindset of becoming a content creator who shares ideas and provides value so that you can then reach out to more people at scale through social media. It's also practice for getting better at your pitch because now, your pitch is not just one-to-one, where you're popping onto a phone call and conversing with either one person or a small group behind closed doors to deliver your sales pitch. Now, you've got to consider the ideas of social media platforms and how people consume content and figure out how you can translate your value proposition into helpful information in the format people consume on social media.

The most crucial component is video. Vertical video is what's driving growth engines behind all the social media platforms. What do you have to do to be successful in that format? A sales pitch on a Zoom call can be done within whatever timeframe the other person will give you, but in the video, you have five seconds to grab their attention. This isn't too far off from what my old sales manager used to tell me when we were doing phone sales. How do you hook the person on the other end of the phone in five seconds or less? We usually used humor. But now you're communicating in one direction with video.

You have to hook people in the first five seconds. How do you do that? The best content marketers always start from the perspective of giving away their best secrets for free. A lot of service professionals or coaches fancy themselves as business strategists. They want to keep their best tips, tricks, and tactics for the people paying them. Look at somebody like Jocko Willink; he gives away a tremendous amount of value upfront with no questions asked and no monetization strategy. He'll deliver two or three hours of excellent content for free. Then, he lists the different things he does at the end of the video, with the idea that you might support him. If you don't support him at this point, you feel like a freeloader.

Give away your best tips, tricks, strategies, and information. You have to give that stuff away for free, and you will find that when you give away your best stuff and add value to the people who are consuming your content, one of two things will happen. They'll be overwhelmed by the information, and it'll be so good that they may try to take pieces of it, but they won't be able to implement it. Now, they've got to come back to you with instructions on implementing and executing. An example would be giving away an excellent component or chapter of your book. If they love it, they will return and spend the full $20 to buy your book.

Or you give away fantastic value, and they want to learn more or deep dive into the topic you gave away in a 5-minute video. Now they're going to sign up for your online course, or they're going to join your virtual coaching program where they can hop on a Zoom call and ask you questions, or they're going to book an hour of your time as a consultant, or they're going to hire you as a service provider, rather than try and replicate all the things that you're telling them to do. They'd hire you instead to do it for them; that's much easier.

That's how you monetize attention when you're putting out great content. You can't be long-winded and pontificating. You have to skip ahead to the good part. That's one thing I picked up in screenwriting when I studied the subject in college. That has always stuck with me as a storyteller. They always told us in class that you should start a scene late and exit early. Instead of starting with a long-winded preamble, jump into the meat of some topic and hit somebody with something right out of the gate that will draw them in, keep them engaged, and keep them watching.

You also get out of that content fast. End it quickly, and then let people know what you will teach them in the following video. Then they have a reason to stick around, and you're not giving away everything in one video. They've got a reason to subscribe, follow you, or stick around. I've been seeing it in my video content, where, between LinkedIn, Instagram, and TikTok, I reach close to 6,000 people a week by putting out my thought leadership across those platforms. Before that, I was just going out cold, trying to meet people by shooting emails into the dark, which is a lot less effective because the AI is doing that on your behalf now at such a volume that you can't compete. You've got to put content out there and allow people to find it in an organic way that doesn't feel unwanted. Instead, pull those people into you.

Takeaways from Chapter 5:

- Consider creating a podcast or other content platform to facilitate deeper connections with prospects and industry leaders.
- Share your expertise generously without expectation of immediate return
- Document your journey authentically rather than creating a polished but inauthentic persona.
- Use content to demonstrate your thinking process and values, not just your capabilities.

6

CHAPTER 6

Build an informant network

The advice to "build an informant network" might sound a little cagey (and maybe it is). However, I enjoy rewatching old episodes of *Mad Men* and thinking about their tactics relating to the modern version of the media, marketing, and advertising world, where we're doing everything digitally. I love seeing how things were done in the old days. They had phones and typewriters. There was no Internet. So, what was their creative process?

When you build media plans, you only create creatives for TV, print, and audio channels. This is fascinating to me as a student of creative advertising. One of my hobbies is going to pawn shops, antique stores, and yard sales to collect vintage ads. I frame the ones that I love and hang them around my house. Since I'm also a massive student of *Mad Men*, I wonder: what did the account guys do to get business? How did these guys get out there and network and meet people, pre-email, pre-social media, and pre-LinkedIn? What was the job like back then? Don Draper is great, but the stars of that show for me were Ken Cosgrove, Roger Sterling, and Pete Campbell.

One of the things that I learned from Roger, if you remember Season 6, Episode 6, is that Roger Sterling had the gate host of the executive lounge for TWA Airlines on the payroll, and if somebody was coming through New York. They were a heavy hitter in marketing, then Roger would jump in a cab and buy a seat next to them on an airline, and he'd jump on a first-class flight so he could sit next to the chief marketing officer of Ford. I've been able to do a version of that here in San Diego, where I meet people at restaurants and always give them my card. I let them know what I do. And I say, 'If you're ever aware of executives coming through, doing private dinners for marketing purposes, and you let me know, I'll ensure you get a nice tip next time I come in.'

I do that with the meeting planners at local hotels. I've got a whole network of informants in San Diego, so I'll usually get a tip anytime something interesting happens in the marketing world. Recently, Southwest was in town for their annual convention. It was called the Southwest Rally. That will never appear on Eventbrite, Facebook, or even Google because it's a private event for Southwest employees. I got a tip from an informant at the San Diego Convention Center that Southwest was in town. Then, I was able to email all my contacts at Southwest, hit them all up, and say, "I see you guys are in town for the rally. If you want to get lunch or coffee while you're in town, I'd be glad to say hi!" That was an extremely relevant outreach to them, and they got back to me. Then, I had a call two weeks later with an executive at Southwest because they had been in town, and that came in as a tip from an informant. We can learn much from the Don Drapers and the Roger Sterlings of yore.

Go out there and build a network of people who can give you helpful information about when and where exciting people will be coming to your area. Building an informant network, cultivating relationships with key gatekeepers, and leveraging that intelligence to create serendipitous opportunities are the strategies that separate the good from the great in business development. Staying current with your network is essential. When I'm not answering emails and making calls, I go through my 30,000 connections on LinkedIn and sort them in different ways based on geography and interest. I'm disconnecting from people who are no longer relevant–maybe they've retired or ultimately left the industry–to make room for new connections at the top of the funnel. It's about constantly connecting with people with no agenda other than getting to know them, building personal relationships, and seeing where the world takes us.

In a world where people depend on inbound marketing or traditional channels that used to work great, like email, AI bots are taking over, making it more cluttered and more complicated to reach new people. The most significant place to start is with warm relationships. Even if you haven't talked to somebody in 13 years, if they remember you and had a good experience, they're generally more willing to take a call or meeting than someone cold.

LinkedIn is an excellent tool for mapping your network and seeing what first-degree connections you share with people who could refer you. It's a tried-and-true tactic of leveraging your network to get intros. Still, not enough attention is paid to how you operationalize that and make it part of your daily routine, connecting with people to give them updates on what you're working on and what they're working on, and building that network of people who are constantly pinging you and referring you to friends as potential colleagues.

Prioritization

Beyond Dunbar's anthropological findings, recent network theory research by Dr. Ronald Burt at the University of Chicago has identified what he calls "structural holes" in professional networks—gaps between different clusters where information doesn't naturally flow. His studies across multiple industries found that professionals who position themselves as bridges across these gaps (essentially becoming information brokers) receive promotions faster, earn higher compensation, and generate more value for their organizations. This research validates my A/B/C approach to relationship prioritization—by strategically identifying relationship investments that bridge structural holes, you create outsized value from limited relationship capital.

So why would we leave the number one thing in our lives, the ultimate predictor of success (our relationships), up to random chance with no degree of prioritization? I recently had JJ on my podcast. He's the recruiter who brought me on at Social Standard, so it is back to an A-level relationship now. Still, he had been in a B-level relationship with me for a while. When you're top of mind with JJ, he sends you more exciting information and referrals. It's always nice to be on the top of the mental Rolodex with recruiters because if you want to be considered for significant roles, those are the people you need to know. But by bringing him onto my podcast, I can make a connection and a touch point with JJ, which ticks that box off the list. As of this morning, 800 people from my network have seen that episode on LinkedIn and spent some time engaging with it and watching or starting the video.

So, 800 people from my network are now exposed to the conversation I had with JJ, and they're seeing my face pop up in their LinkedIn feed with another super connector. And it's funny: there are the people in my network, my 30,000 on LinkedIn (and that's one level where there are A's, B's, and C's, and I can't control how the algorithm serves up and shows people), but what I can optimize for is the Venn diagram between my connections, my network, and my guest's network, where it intersects and clashes, right? So if I invite JJ to my podcast, then I also post it, and I tag JJ, and he engages with my podcast, but then takes it a step deeper, shares it on his social network, and then gets engagement from his network, which does two things. JJ's social media endorsement adds new potential folks to my network who are seeing me for the first time. They can watch our conversation to get to know me, but they will probably watch it more because they want to see what JJ says. But by association, they will also see what I have to say. The real sweet spot is where my network intersects with JJ's. The people in the Venn diagram of our combined networks who know me and know JJ is a double touchpoint. Those people probably engaged with the show, shared it, or reached out to me because they saw JJ on my podcast or the post that he shared. You want to have a force ranking system to figure out the most critical relationships in your life from a professional perspective. You want to do that because you want to prioritize how you engage with those people and set metrics around how you will connect with them.

Early in my career, in my twenties, I approached networking, especially in the media and entertainment industry, with an expense account and a bar to go to. My version of being a good sales rep then was, let's travel, get clients out of the office, and get them into social situations such as bars, sporting events, fancy dinners, and Dodgers and Lakers games. Get them into situations involving social lubrication (i.e., alcohol) to get everybody's guard down and have a good time. A degree of bonding happens over being out there and partying. That's the stereotypical salesperson that goes on benders and has a good time and treats everybody, and look, in your twenties, when there's a bunch of media planners at the agencies who are also in their twenties, that makes sense. There probably is a period in your life and a style of rep that you want to hire who can talk to that specific audience, who can speak to that young twenties age demographic that just wants to get treated to nights out for happy hour because they're practically making minimum wage at media agencies.

I always joke that media agencies don't pay entry-level careers that well, but the benefits are great. Guys like me and reps out there give them perks, take them out, and subsidize their personal lives by wielding their expense accounts, and that's great because it adds some value to them. But genuine bonds were formed over partying, which caught up with me in my life.

I was ultimately doing way too much. There were situations where I turned off relationships instead of building them because I took them too far. Not to mention, if you're a good salesperson and have that unlimited expense account, you can go out drinking and partying every night of the week. That eventually catches up with you, just as it caught up with me. I was at this point in my life where I was saying that was the last straw of why I wasn't quitting alcohol, because I thought I couldn't be a business development person without drinking, and that was part and parcel of it.

So what I would do is I would come here to California, and I'd be sober when I was here and home with my family, but when I traveled to New York or Chicago, I would drink on the road. Eventually, that caught up with me, and I met somebody who changed my mindset. I'm not going to name them because people's relationship with alcohol is a personal and private matter, but he was very successful in the same role as me, and he had been sober for over 20 years.

That stuck with me. He said, "Hey, look, Dylan, you know you are in your early thirties. You've got a young family. You've got a wife. Use that to your advantage. It's time for you to elevate your prospecting from the 20-year-old entry-level subset that doesn't have any power at the end of the day. They may be the gateway, but they'll ultimately have to go to others for decision-making sign-off anyway."

He told me, "It's time to step up your game. You should now prospect for people at a life stage similar to yours. People who are married, have young families, peel off after work, catch the train, and go home to their kids, and your prospecting should change. You won't invite them to the bar anymore. You'll invite them to the golf course, the shooting range, the yoga class, the rock climbing gym, the cool coffee shop, the cool new restaurant in town, or the cool comedy show. You know, things where you don't have to drink and party, and they'll be grateful that you just want to hang out, have a good time, build a relationship, and they don't have to wake up the next day with a hangover."

So I started to do that. I began to set my sights not only longitudinally, directly on people in their thirties, but I also started aiming a little higher—people in their forties and even their fifties. I could relate to a different type of prospect: building a family. When I started to meet people in their forties and fifties who had kids of a similar age, I began to figure out ways we could integrate them. My perspective as a salesperson nowadays is that I only travel a little if I can incorporate my family. Last year, I attended a handful of conferences by myself and went to Austin and Vegas. I went on four trips last year by myself. I brought my family to all the other conferences I attended. I am usually very intentional and specific about picking opportunities to travel and bring my family so they can enjoy the resort, or we can tack on a vacation, or get in the RV and do a road trip. Still, I'm doing sales meetings along the way.

There's a refreshing work-life balance component to this approach. Integrating your family will create a stickier bond with the people you're spending time with because your kids are getting to know each other. Your spouses are getting to know each other. So it's not just a guy's thing; they can do the same thing. They can spend their vacation time with somebody they know professionally, which, generally, we wouldn't be able to get away with, and just do a guy's trip whenever we wanted, without bringing the family along.

My kids go to a homeschool co-op, and there are daily drop-offs and pick-ups. There are fundraisers, daddy-daughter dances, and all these different activities around my kids' school, and I then get to meet other professional people. For example, Rob Machado's son attends my kids' homeschool co-op. So, those are opportunities for me to meet other parents and dads and get to know them and what they do. I also do a program called Adventure Guides through the YMCA, where a hundred dads and about 250 girls camp in San Diego County once a month. I am camping with a hundred other dads for a weekend. I met a guy who launched the cannabis brand for the Grateful Dead, so that's very relevant to the branding and marketing world. It's relevant to me, and we've also become mountain biking friends.

Another guy in my tribe was the operations person for the Warped Tour. Action sports, marketing, and experiential events are similar to the work I've done with Adobe, Tony Hawk, and the World Surf League, so you can't be too intentional because you just never know who you'll meet at these things. Still, you can pick and stack your activities in a way that allows you to build community. For me and my kids, I don't tell my daughters, "Hey, you're going to go do this thing because I want to meet other dads." But if it's something that they express interest in and want to do, and I can help empower them, plus I get to meet people through it, awesome. My youngest daughter is modeling, so when she shows up and does a photo shoot for an emerging clothing brand here in San Diego, getting to know the brand's owner is probably an excellent strategic priority for my wife and me.

Match your life stage, your passions, and the things you're interested in, and incorporate that level of currency components into your networking. I'm attending a networking event I found for tomorrow, a 3-hour pickleball event for entrepreneurs, which only costs 20 bucks. I get to go out and cross another thing off my list, which is exercise, and I'm going to find some like-minded folks who are into pickleball and are all entrepreneurs. That's way better, in my opinion, than going to some bar, a happy hour, or even a luncheon because I'm going to go out and I'm going to sweat. I'm going to do something with people who are like-minded and have a hobby that I'm interested in. I'll cross off three different buckets with that event. I have a like-minded association with sports; I enjoy pickleball. I would go to a pickleball event just with friends, or I would go to a pickleball event that didn't even have anything to do with networking. That's a level of mutual interest, like sports. But then, take that to the next level and add the family component: do things with your kids or spouse. Find activities. I use Google and Facebook events to find more generic types of activities that are separate from business.

Always think about how you can live your most extraordinary life, but at the same time, push your business agenda forward with every move you make. Thinking of every moment of your life as a business development opportunity may sound tiring. Still, if you genuinely love it and truly love meeting people, you love the activities you're doing. And you get to do it with your spouse and kids. That's the perfect flow state. You're getting to do business and life in tandem instead of thinking of those things as separate, disjointed things.

In 1907, J.P. Morgan proved that sometimes the most powerful moves in business come from the relationships you've built over decades. The U.S. was facing a massive financial crisis—banks were failing left and right, and there wasn't yet a Federal Reserve to step in and help. Morgan didn't just throw money at the problem. He used his relationships. He locked the heads of New York's most prominent banks in his library and wouldn't let them leave until they agreed to work together to save the financial system. That only worked because Morgan had spent decades building trust with those people. They weren't just business contacts; they trusted his judgment and knew he was looking at the bigger picture. What's worth remembering is how Morgan used "quiet influence." He didn't make public speeches or try to grab headlines. Instead, he worked through his network, using personal conversations and private meetings to get things done. He understood that real influence comes from trust built over time, not from making the most noise.

The three depths of networking

Think of your network as ocean layers: surface level, middle depth, and deep waters. Each layer serves a purpose, and you must be intentional about operating at each level.

- Surface Level: The Connection Points

THIS IS YOUR LINKEDIN NETWORK, conference contacts, and industry acquaintances. I've got thousands of these connections, and while they might seem shallow, they're crucial. They're like having sonar in the ocean—they help you detect opportunities and stay aware of what's happening in your industry.

For example, I track about 5,000 people in my broader network through LinkedIn and my CRM. I don't have deep relationships with all of them. Still, when I see someone post about a new job or a company announcement, it gives me valuable intelligence about market movements and potential opportunities.

- [Middle Depth: The Cultivation Zone]()

THIS IS where the real work happens. You're actively nurturing these relationships—maybe 50-100 people at any given time. They're beyond surface level but not yet your inner circle. Think of them like coral reefs—they need regular attention and the right conditions to thrive.

I had a middle-depth relationship with a marketing director at a major brand. We'd meet quarterly for coffee, share industry insights, and occasionally help each other with introductions. Over the years, this steady cultivation paid off when she became CMO at a different company and brought us in as their primary agency. The key was consistency without pressure—I never tried to force the relationship deeper than it naturally wanted.

- Deep Waters: Your Inner Circle

These are your 10-15 key relationships—the ones you invest in heavily and go beyond business with. Like deep-sea creatures, these relationships operate under different rules than the surface ones. They require more energy and attention but yield the most remarkable results.

Remember Jayson from Adobe? That relationship went deep because we both allowed it to. We shared personal struggles, celebrated each other's wins, and supported each other through tough times. When you operate at this depth, business becomes secondary to human connection.

Here's how I manage each level:

Surface Level Management:

- Regular but automated check-ins through CRM
- Social media engagement
- Quarterly mass updates or newsletters
- Event-based outreach

Middle Depth Cultivation:

- Monthly personal check-ins
- Customized value sharing
- Regular face-to-face meetings
- Intentional relationship-building activities

Deep Water Investment:

- Weekly or bi-weekly contact
- Family integration when appropriate
- Shared experiences outside of business
- Long-term life and career support

These three levels of networking—surface, middle, and deep—correspond directly to the going deep framework we established earlier. They represent a progressive movement from contact to context to connection, with your inner circle relationships reaching the community center of truly integrated networks. The trick is knowing which relationships belong at which depth and intentionally moving them between levels. Not every surface connection needs to go deep, and not every deep connection starts that way. It's about recognizing potential and nurturing it appropriately.

Grow your network before you need it

As a student at UCSB, I joined a fraternity called Sigma Chi. It was a social experience, with a lot of partying and a great time overall. One of the jobs that I got when I was in the fraternity was as alumni chairman. My responsibility was to plan a reunion and ensure that we communicated with the 1,200 alumni from my chapter at UC Santa Barbara about what was happening at the fraternity. Before I inherited that job, let's just say it could have been handled better. Our typical version of Alumni Weekend was a keg. We dropped it in the backyard, and if anybody showed up, they showed up, and if they didn't, they didn't. And the guys that usually did show up were pretty pissed and disappointed that we put zero effort into it.

Over the years that I lived in the fraternity house, occasionally, guys would stop by late at night or when they were in town with their wives and wanted to see the chapter house, or maybe there was a wedding in Santa Barbara they were in town for. They just wanted to come to the fraternity house and see how things were going. I had gotten a handful of business cards, maybe three or four, from guys who had stopped by throughout the years and said hello. When I became the alum chair, we needed more information for our 1,200 alums. I took those 3 or 4 cards, emailed each, and said, "I know we haven't done an excellent job communicating with you before, but I want to improve things. I'd love to start my tenure by reestablishing communication. I need to get everybody's email address. Would you four guys give me the email addresses of all your pledge brothers and friends so I can grow that list?"

Those four guys sent me 15 emails, and I asked them to do the same. Those 15 emails turned into 40 emails, which I rinsed and repeated. Before you knew it, I was in touch with 600 of our 1,200 living alums. All of a sudden, cool stuff started happening. Guys would drop off a pool table they weren't using anymore or just drop checks in the mail. That was my first experience in seeing that when you build a network, you're laying the foundation for people to reconnect and communicate with each other. If you are a part of that foundation, good things will flow back to you. When I graduated from college, I wanted to have the same experience in the professional world, so when I arrived in LA, I joined the Sigma Chi Alumni chapter, became the social chairman, and started a subgroup called Sigs in Entertainment.

There, I did the same thing. I trolled LinkedIn and any alum database for any information about any Sigma Chi who worked in the entertainment industry. Sigma Chi was stacked with heavy hitters like David Letterman, Tom Selleck, and Brad Pitt. I would find whoever I could and use that information to create connections with more Sigma Chis who were working in the entertainment industry. Those in the entertainment industry know that everything is about who you know. So in pretty short order, we had connected with a bunch of the heavy hitters: guys from Michael Connelly, the author of *The Lincoln Lawyer* and the *Bosch* series of books, to Stephen J. Cannell, who created or co-created 40 of the classic network television shows (such as *The A-Team*, *Rockford Files*, and *21 Jump Street*).

Then we started doing a monthly hangout where I would pick a venue in Los Angeles, and we would all meet up together, network, and have a drink and dinner together. That's why and how I reached out initially and met Nate, the co-author of this book, through that exact process over 13 years ago. I wasn't in a business development role then in my career; I was in a low-level development job at a reality television production company called Nash. My days were busy; sometimes I was busy all day, but sometimes I got my whole slate of projects done in the first hour of work, and then I just would have nothing but time to work on projects. I write and do research, but I mainly build my network. I just built this network from scratch. I did this diligently for three years.

I never asked for anything. But there did come a day when I found that I was at the end of my road with Nash. From an earnings and title perspective, I knew there was a ceiling on what I could do. It wasn't going to be the place that was going to get me to where I wanted to go in my career. So, with one email, I sent a note to the Sigma Chi network in the entertainment industry that I had helped cultivate throughout the last few years. In short order, a guy named Kirk got me an interview to work on Oprah Winfrey's profile production show called *The Big Give*. I went in, and I had a great interview. I got a job offer to be a segment producer, and that job helped me skip a bunch of rungs in the production world. I doubled my salary in that one move.

That is just one example. You have connections even if you're not a business development person or salesperson. Whether that is your church, fraternity, sorority, civics club, sports league, the parents of your kids' friends, or an alumni association from where you went to school, there are ways that you can build a network of like-minded professionals. The idea is to grow and nurture that network without expecting anything to return to you. When you give and create without having expectations, if the day comes when you need to leverage it, it will deliver for you above and beyond your wildest dreams.

Your network is a muscle

Think of your network as a muscle. It only becomes powerful when you train with it and use it. Suppose you leave your network, LinkedIn database, or CRM on the shelf, collecting dust because you're living in a scarcity mindset. In that case, relationships are like poker chips that are only traded around when there's something in it for you. That is a great way to make your network atrophy. This was one of many lessons I learned while working for Keith Ferrazzi. When you flex your network, if you touch base with your network often enough and provide introductions within your network and connect people, that's essentially the heavy lifting–or the exercise of networking. It's about creating more connections in the spiderweb of relationships.

I have always tried to operate from the rule of three: If I go and meet with somebody, I'm always trying to figure out what three introductions I can make for them that are valuable to them. We've all received introductions that waste our time, and I try to be thoughtful and generous in those situations. Still, if I get introduced to another financial planner, I'll probably pull my hair out. Specific introductions should be more relevant and focused on the brand. Not all introductions are welcome. In a meeting, you must also be very aware and ask yourself, "What would be strategically valuable for this person? Listen and figure out *what these people are looking for.*

Listening is a crucial point. You have to be listening for qualifications. What home run introductions are going to be valuable for people? There are levels of introduction that come with different components of currency. There's the level of professional currency, "I'm looking for a social media manager," and you can introduce somebody who might be a good fit, and they'll be a good employee. Then, some items, like sales accounts, relate to business development and impact the bottom line. The next level is personal: "I can make introductions that would be relevant for his kids to get placed in a job or at the right school that they're trying to attend," or something for them. The highest level is physical and spiritual. "He's going through back pain," and I introduced him to a physical therapist or a chiropractor who changed his life and health situation, or I introduced him to a personal trainer who helped him lose weight. I brought him to church, and he now has meaning.

There are levels of introductions that also flow up and down what Keith Ferrazzi called the currency pyramid. At the top are health and spirituality, and at the bottom are professional and personal. "You guys should connect because you could go golfing."

If I can think of the most essential introduction that anybody's ever made for me, it's a mutual friend of Nate's and mine named JJ, whom I mentioned earlier. As a headhunter, he is a master at connecting and building relationships. He's the only person in 15 years who has convinced me to move companies. Another strategic introduction that JJ made for me was when we were at SXSW, and I had been traveling back and forth to my office from San Diego to LA. It was becoming very taxing on my family. It was a lot of time back and forth, many nights away from the family, and commuting by car three hours each way.

JJ heard me complaining about this commute while we were at an event. He mentioned that he knows someone in Carlsbad who has a plane. The guy lives in Carlsbad but works in Santa Monica. This man was Phil Dixon, and he's the COO of K2 Games, but more importantly for this story, he's a pilot. He has a four-seat plane and would give me a ride when traveling back and forth. I thought it was quite an expense to buy a plane and learn to fly just so you could skip the traffic to LA, but Phil is an analytical guy. He had spreadsheets explaining why it made sense to purchase a plane. This wasn't an ego thing. He taught me an important lesson that day. What is your time worth? How many hours would you save not sitting in traffic for six hours, five days a week? How much value is that time back at home with your family? Owning a plane, a boat, or an RV isn't about having cool toys. That's a benefit for sure, but what it means is freedom. Freedom to live where you want, but being able to work in any city within a short flight away. The ability to say, "Should we have lunch in Catalina today? Or how about Vegas? We can be there in an hour." That mindset stuck with me.

Then JJ introduced me to him, and because JJ is good at what he does, Phil, with no questions asked, said that I could ride along with him on his next business trip.

He'd never met me, but Phil said, "No problem. Just show up at the airport at 6:30 AM."

I was like, *what? Are you kidding me?* I arrived at the airport and asked if I could pitch in on gas. I am still determining what jet fuel costs, but I'd gladly pitch in. He told me that since he's a personal pilot and not a professional pilot, taking any gas money from me would be against the law because he'd be chartering the plane. All he charged me was a cup of black coffee from Starbucks. I went to Starbucks early and ensured his order was dialed in and ready.

When I showed up, I met Phil at the Carlsbad airport. We got into his little 4-seater plane. Cirrus are like a motorcycle with wings. It's not a jet; it's a legit turbo prop plane where the only place to sit is up front with the pilot. I remember it was blue on white, like the Corvettes from the '80s that I always dreamed of driving. We were casually dressed, not quite like pilots, not quite like we were about to walk into the boardroom. The take-off was exhilarating, especially when Phil asked me to pull the throttle and get us into the air when we hit the end of the runway.

Within 30 minutes, door to door, from Carlsbad Airport to Santa Monica Airport, we were on the ground. He was heading to the office where he worked, and I walked to my office in 25 minutes. It was the best commute of my life. Then, on the way home, he even let me take the wheel for a little bit. I've never been in the pilot's seat of a plane in my entire life, yet he was willing to let a stranger ride in this plane and take the wheel. This was all based on the power of JJ's introduction.

This shows the power of the currency that a guy like JJ has. If he introduces you to somebody, people assume they're good and worthwhile people to know, so they would be willing to give you a ride in their private plane. This can work in the opposite direction as well. I contacted JJ recently to ask him to introduce me to somebody because I wanted to do business with them. I knew that he had been trying to recruit their head of sales a few years before. I knew he had a relationship there and asked him for an introduction.

His response was, "Guy's a scumbag. Don't use my name."

Burning a relationship in your network, especially with a well-respected super-connector like JJ, can tarnish your brand for life.

Not only did JJ say, "Absolutely not," He said, "I will not introduce you, even though you need their capability, but I can introduce you to someone else who does the same thing."

He mentioned that Vince Thompson had a company in his portfolio with a similar capability. Thus, Jim steered me to a more trusted resource for the same outcome I was searching for, rather than letting me do business with someone he felt was untrustworthy.

The six degrees of separation are always in effect. As trite and uninteresting as it may sound on the surface, there is a reason many cliches are true: always be careful with your reputation. Be kind and treat others with respect. Engaging with your network should be seen as something other than a sporadic activity pursued only in times of need, but as an ongoing investment. Interactions and exchanges should be approached to add value, reinforce trust, and deepen connections. This approach enriches our professional journeys and ensures that our network is robust, responsive, and reciprocally beneficial when opportunities arise.

Andrew Carnegie and Henry Frick met in 1881 in New York City while the Frick's were on their honeymoon. They started as the perfect business partners. Carnegie had the vision for building a steel empire, and Frick had the operational genius to make it happen. They complemented each other perfectly and built the largest steel company in the world. As their business got bigger, their relationship got shallower. They stopped having the honest conversations that had made their partnership work. Everything became about the next deal, the subsequent acquisition. They stopped investing in their relationship.

The result? One of the most spectacular business breakups in history. These guys went from partners to enemies, nearly destroying what they'd built together. The lesson isn't just "be nice to your business partners." It's that you have to keep investing in relationships, even when—

especially when—things are going well. You can't just coast on past success. The irony is that if they'd maintained the depth of their early relationship—if they'd kept having those honest conversations and maintained a genuine connection—they might have worked through their differences. Instead, they let their relationship become transactional, and that's when everything fell apart. This is why I always tell people: the depth of your business relationships isn't just about being successful today; it's about building something that can last through the tough times. Carnegie and Frick built an empire together, but they forgot to maintain the foundation of trust and genuine connection that made it all possible in the first place.

Repairing damaged trust isn't just an art—it's been studied extensively by organizational psychologists. Dr. Roy Lewicki's research at Ohio State University identified what he calls the "Wheel of Trust Repair," consisting of six essential elements: acknowledge the violation, explain what happened, express genuine remorse, make reparations, demonstrate reformed behavior, and request forgiveness. What's particularly interesting is that his studies found that the sequence matters tremendously. This research validates what I've learned through painful experiences: when I've damaged trust with clients, jumping straight to explanations or solutions without first acknowledging the impact rarely works. The fastest path to relationship recovery isn't bypassing the difficult conversations—it's moving through them with intentionality and the proper sequence.

In studies of business relationships, Lewicki found that properly repaired relationships often ended up more potent than those that never experienced a breach. The shared experience of working through a challenging situation created what he called "resilient trust"—trust that has been tested and purposefully rebuilt. Of course, this relationship-building is happening in an increasingly digital world. I'm not one of those who think AI and automation will replace human connection. However, we must intentionally use technology to enhance rather than replace authentic relationships.

Takeaways from Chapter 6:

- Build an "informant network" that helps you identify relationship opportunities in your key geographic areas.
- Leverage membership in community organizations to establish common ground with new connections.
- Treat your network as a muscle that requires regular exercise through meaningful engagement.
- Grow your network before you need it - Invest in relationship development without immediate business goals.

CHAPTER 7

From AI to Fish Tacos

On my podcast, I recently interviewed Brady Brim-DeForest, Chief Operations Officer of FormulaAI at MediaMonks. Our conversation about AI's impact on sales crystallized my perspective on technology's role in relationship-building.

The question on everyone's mind is straightforward: Will AI replace salespeople? I believe the answer is equally straightforward—no, but it will transform how we work. Rather than eliminating the need for human connection, AI will enhance our capacity to create it by handling routine tasks that consume our time and attention. AI excels at research, personalization, and pattern recognition—capabilities that can significantly enhance relationship-building when adequately leveraged. Tools like CopyAI and Claude can draft personalized outreach that sounds more natural than generic templates. Platforms like Lavender.ai can analyze email effectiveness and suggest improvements based on your historical performance with different prospect types. Solutions like Gong can identify patterns in successful sales conversations that might otherwise take years to recognize.

What's crucial is understanding that these tools serve relationship-building rather than replace it. AI can find connection points between you and a prospect, but you must determine how to make those points relevant and meaningful. It can generate a first draft, but you must infuse it with authentic voice and perspective. It can schedule follow-ups, but you must show up as a complete human when those connections occur. The counterbalance to increasing AI adoption is a deeper human connection. As technology handles more routine aspects of sales, our distinctive value comes from what AI cannot replicate: genuine curiosity, emotional intelligence, ethical judgment, and authentic relationship-building. This creates an interesting paradox—the more AI advances, the more valuable human interaction becomes.

This means developing a dual expertise for today's sales professionals: mastering AI tools to enhance efficiency while deepening interpersonal skills that create meaningful connections. The most successful approach isn't resisting AI or surrendering to it but strategically integrating it into a human-centered approach to sales. When AI handles research, drafting, scheduling, and analysis, we gain additional capacity for the deep listening, thoughtful questioning, and genuine connection that only humans can provide. AI might help you fill your calendar with meetings, but the quality of those interactions—and the depth of the relationships they build—will remain distinctly human.

It's tempting to think technology can handle all the "relationship maintenance" while we focus on other things. But I've learned that technology works best when it handles the logistics of relationships, not the relationships themselves. I test and play with every tech tool out there. My CRM tracks interactions, AI helps draft initial outreach, and automation ensures I don't drop important balls. But I never pretend that these tools are building relationships for me. They're freeing up time and mental space so I can focus on the real work of human connection. Think of it as a dinner party. Technology can help you manage the guest list, send invitations, and remind you to buy groceries. But it can't create the warmth of conversation around your table. It can't generate spontaneous moments of connection when people let their guard down. It can't build trust.

I've watched too many people hide behind technology, using it as a substitute for genuine interaction. The most valuable use of technology in relationship building is the opposite of what most people think. Instead of automating interactions, use it to identify opportunities for real connection. When my CRM alerts me that I haven't spoken to someone in a while, I don't send an automated check-in. I think about that person, what's happening, and how I might add value to their day. Sometimes, that means picking up the phone when everyone else would send an email.

The future isn't about replacing human connection with technology. It's about using technology to make more space for human connection. Every minute saved by automation is a minute you can spend in a real conversation. Every task AI handles is mental energy you can devote to understanding someone's needs and challenges. This isn't just philosophical, it's practical. In a world where everyone tries to automate relationships, genuine human connection becomes even more valuable. The ability to step away from the screen and have a real conversation, truly listen and understand,

and build trust through consistent, authentic interaction–these skills matter more, not less, in our digital age.

The real magic happens in the messy, imperfect human moments that no algorithm can replicate. Think about your closest business relationships. I bet none of them started with a perfectly crafted email. Mine certainly didn't. Take my relationship with Jayson at Adobe: it all started with a LinkedIn message that broke every "best practice" rule. But it was genuine, and that made all the difference.

The rise of digital tools has created an interesting paradox in relationship building. The easier it becomes to "connect" with someone, the harder it becomes to form genuine connections. Marc Benioff, the founder of Salesforce, understood this early on. While building a company that would revolutionize digital sales relationships, he simultaneously invested heavily in creating in-person experiences. His annual Dreamforce conference wasn't just about showcasing products. What Benioff got right, and what many miss, is that digital tools should enhance rather than replace human interaction. When Salesforce launched, many predicted that face-to-face sales would become obsolete. Instead, the most successful salespeople learned to use digital tools to make in-person interactions more meaningful and targeted.

When the pandemic hit in 2020, Ben Horowitz of Andreessen Horowitz faced a fundamental challenge: maintaining the firm's relationship-driven approach to venture capital in a world where face-to-face meetings were impossible. Their solution wasn't simply to move everything to video calls but to completely rethink how technology could facilitate real connection. In his book *The Hard Thing About Hard Things*, Horowitz had already written about the importance of in-person interaction. But when circumstances forced a change, he discovered that video could unexpectedly deepen relationships. By seeing into people's homes, meeting their families (often unintentionally), and sharing the universal experience of navigating a crisis, many business relationships became more personal, not less.

The lesson isn't that video calls are better than in-person meetings—they're not. It's that any technology, when used thoughtfully, can create opportunities for deeper connection. The key is to use the tool to add rather than remove.

The human algorithm

To be clear, I'm not suggesting we abandon digital tools—they're essential for maintaining connections at scale. What I am saying is that we need to understand their limitations. Digital tools excel at maintaining relationships and sharing information efficiently, but they cannot substitute for face-to-face interaction's neurological and psychological impact. The most effective approach is to use digital tools strategically to enhance, not replace, in-person connection.

Research confirms this intuitive truth. UCLA's Matthew Lieberman has demonstrated through brain-imaging studies that our brains fundamentally process in-person social interaction differently than digital interaction. Face-to-face conversations activate neural pathways associated with deeper emotional processing and memory formation, explaining why a one-hour coffee meeting creates a stronger impression than dozens of email exchanges. Similarly, Dr. Paul Zak's research on oxytocin (the "trust hormone") reveals that in-person interaction typically generates a significantly stronger neurochemical response than virtual communication. His studies found that video calls produce about 80% of the oxytocin response of in-person meetings, phone calls generate around 50%, and emails/texts substantially less.

This science explains something I've observed repeatedly in my career: even the best CRM system can't replace the intuition developed from years of face-to-face interactions. Technology can help you remember birthdays, track touchpoints, and identify patterns, but it can't build trust—that still happens human to human. Business leaders who understand this balance between technology and humanity effectively. When Lou Gerstner took over IBM in 1993, the company had become distant from its customers. His first move wasn't implementing new technology but getting IBM's leaders in front of customers again. Similarly, Microsoft's Satya Nadella, while leading one of the world's largest technology companies, maintains that the most critical conversations still happen face-to-face. Even Zoom's founder, Eric Yuan, emphasized the importance of in-person connection while creating a platform that would make remote meetings ubiquitous.

DIGITAL TOOLS EXCEL AT:

- Maintaining regular touch-points
- Sharing information efficiently
- Tracking relationship history
- Identifying patterns and opportunities

BUT HUMAN INTERACTION is irreplaceable for:

- Building and maintaining trust

- Navigating complex negotiations
- Handling sensitive situations
- Deepening relationships

THE KEY IS ORCHESTRATING them effectively. As AI and automation advance, the more our world digitizes, the more valuable genuine human connection becomes. Every automated touchpoint makes authentic human interaction stand out more distinctly. The goal isn't to replace human connection but to enhance it by using technology to create more space for authentic engagement. This approach requires constant adjustment. What worked in relationship-building five years ago might not work today. Regardless, we should use technology to increase efficiency, not to create distance. In a world where everyone is trying to automate relationships, your most significant differentiator becomes your ability to create genuine human connections.

Pricing transparency

There are many "stroking" people in the advertising and marketing industry. Some people are willing to take calls and talk to almost anybody without any indication of buying a service because they may learn something. Even more nefarious is this whole cattle call RFP culture that's been prevalent since I've been in the advertising industry, where agencies or brands will put out an RFP with no real intention of working with somebody new. They just cattle call a bunch of companies and see who responds and gets free work and free ideas that they're just going to end up handing over to their existing agency. In the influencer space, people will reach out and want to see a talent list. They want to see a roster of people you represent. They'll give you their spec of what they're looking for, but they want you to hand-feed them a list of influencers. Finding the right influencers is one of the hardest things to do in the influencer space. They'll mind-fuck a bunch of agencies and ask them to come up with countless lists for their particular campaign. They'll crowdsource these talent lists from different places. Then, they'll just take those lists and reach out to the influencers independently or through their existing agency.

When I'm upfront about how we structure our costs and where my margins are, it completely changes the dynamic from adversarial haggling to collaborative problem-solving. The research explains why transparency triggers reciprocity, which is fundamental to building trust. When you start negotiating with a prospect or a client and get down to the more complex conversations, like, "Hey, what will this cost me? What am I going to get?" The number one and most important thing is transparency. I've been on many sales calls where I just asked somebody straight out, "What does this cost? I like what you're saying. I want to buy it. Can you tell me what this costs?"

And then they flip it back to me and say, "What's your budget?"

"My budget is what it costs!" Many salespeople like to play this weird chicken-and-egg dance. The industry has trained us to let the other person make the first pitch because we want to ensure we sell ourselves well.

If I say, "This costs $50,000," and somebody had a $100,000 budget, I just lost $50,000 in revenue. That's not true. You can give your pricing a number and make it flexible. Tell people, "This isn't like ordering off a Chinese menu.

This is a consultative sales process." There's another way to structure the cost of influencer marketing: The agency takes 5% to 35% of the revenue as a pass-through. Why is there a significant discrepancy between both ends of the spectrum? What determines 5% versus 35%?

5% is: Are we doing one deal with Kim Kardashian for a million dollars? I can take 50 grand off that, do one transaction, feel good about it, and take a tiny percentage. I gave you value by negotiating a deal with Kim. I charged a minimal fee to make that happen and provided my time and services. On the other end of that spectrum is 35%. If you want me to have 300 influencers post on the same day, all posting a particular piece of creative work, and manage 300 people, that will be on the 35% side. The key is to provide transparency to clients. If you can be transparent with clients and show them that we think about pricing in a standardized way, they will feel that you're not just trying to grab their budget and get everything potentially available.

Clients don't know their budget because they don't know what something costs. I always try to find ways to qualify. It gets them into the mindset of being a buyer. This is especially helpful when you have a SaaS play or are demoing software. Once you get down to qualifying a prospect, I'll ask them: Do you have a brief that you guys are sending out to agency partners where you're articulating what problem you are trying to solve?

What's your timeline? What types of influencers are you thinking of? What platforms do you want? Where are you thinking about using the content? Ask them questions, qualifying that they've thought through the opportunity enough to articulate a brief.

And can they send you that brief or that RFP? That gives you a particular document to respond to, which is the best-case scenario. Clients often say, "Well, no, I haven't written a brief yet."

"What if I walked you through a process that we call a reverse brief? I'll send you a document with a minimum list of questions I need you to answer as specifically as possible. Then I can assemble a proposal for you in a week or less."

Sometimes, they're not quite there. So I'll say, "What if I were to send you a list of influencers? Would that be helpful? Can you at least give me some idea of the types of people that you think you'd want to work with?" I can pop the results into an influencer technology platform, whether CreatorIQ or Tagger, and I can quickly pop in the things they're qualifying for, whether it's demographic data or types of influencers. What Category? I can pipe in as many data components as possible and then quickly spit out a list, giving them something to respond to.

Or they will say, "We don't know what types of influencers we want to work with. We haven't gotten that far." Then, I'll often ask them, "What if I were to send you a case study? Would that be helpful? Can I send you some case studies of other clients who look like you? I can show you what they've done and the results and outcomes that were generated."

Then, you'll build credibility for yourself by suggesting that some other people we've worked with look and feel like their brand. You can then determine whether we've made the proper assessment and whether we've compared you to brands that you think are in your category or relevant.

That will give you some credibility that we've either worked with people you respect, don't respect, or consider competitors. Then, you can see the types of campaigns that they did. Then, they will ask, "How much did Brand X spend on this campaign?" It allows you to jump into that pricing conversation.

Transparency wins the day. Not sharing pricing information with clients on discovery calls will aggravate them. They feel you withhold information to get them to throw out the first pitch so you can hoover up all their money.

I would instead operate from a place of transparency, understanding that all deals are different. And some solutions don't have cookie-cutter formats. You should have some level of pricing and understanding of your product and service, allowing you to establish baselines around how you bill. How you charge and what people get, knowing there will be some customization once you get down the road and get into more specific conversations. In negotiations, people readily share their thoughts on pricing and offerings when you clearly state your position. Transparency in pricing discussions demonstrates the authentic connection element of going deep. It shows you value the relationship more than maximizing the immediate transaction, which paradoxically often leads to more extensive long-term value creation.

The psychology of pricing conversations fascinates me because it reveals so much about trust dynamics. Dr. Robert Cialdini, the godfather of influence psychology, discusses the principle of "reciprocal concessions" in his research. He found that when we make ourselves slightly vulnerable by sharing information first (like being transparent about pricing), the other party feels a psychological obligation to reciprocate with openness. A landmark study from Stanford Business School reinforces this. Researchers found that when salespeople were transparent about potential downsides of their offerings before discussing price, customer trust increased by 76%, and the likelihood of purchase rose by 29%. The researchers called this the "vulnerability loop"—by making yourself vulnerable first, you create space for mutual trust.

You may say, "Sure. This approach sounds great when you're established or selling something in high demand, but what about when you're the underdog?" This objection cuts to the heart of power dynamics in business relationships. When you're a startup competing against established players or selling in a buyer's market, depth may be a luxury you can't afford. The temptation is to take whatever you can get on whatever terms are offered.

Early in my career, I felt this pressure acutely. When I was employee number three at a new agency, competing against global firms with massive resources, I thought I had to accept any terms just to get in the door. However, I quickly learned that operating from this position of weakness created inherently unbalanced and unsustainable relationships. The turning point came when I realized that going deep was even more critical when not in a position of power. When you can't compete on size, resources, or brand recognition, your ability to build genuine human connections becomes your most significant differentiator. I started focusing on prospects where I could add unique value beyond what larger competitors offer. Instead of trying to win on their terms, I changed the game, emphasizing relationship quality, personalized attention, and authentic connection that more prominent firms couldn't match.

For instance, with one early client, I couldn't compete with the lavish entertainment budget of my larger competitors. Instead, I invited the marketing director to join me in volunteering at a beach cleanup—something I knew aligned with her values. That Saturday morning, picking up trash together created a deeper bond than any fancy dinner could have, and it cost nothing but time. Even when you don't have the strongest product or the lowest price, understanding someone's values and creating a genuine human connection gives you an edge that transcends traditional power dynamics.

The generosity effect

How much are you willing to roll up your sleeves and provide value without getting compensated for it?

Sadly, in the agency world, it's almost an expectation to provide something for nothing. We're all familiar with the RFP process, where a brand will invite a group of agencies to pitch, and it can feel like March Madness. You're in there with a group of other agencies, and everybody's bringing the best of their best teams to battle it out and come up with the best ideas. Many times, even if they end up not picking your agency, they can still take your ideas and use them.

It's an antiquated process that performs a casting call from ten times as many companies as the available work. There are a finite number of clients and budgets compared to the endless number of agencies. We're often willing to give a lot of our intellectual capital, and sometimes even our sweat equity, out for free in hopes of attaining further business.

What I've discovered over time is that generosity isn't just a nice ideal—it's a powerful business strategy when applied thoughtfully. I like to operate from a perspective of generosity but with clear boundaries. There are certainly clients willing to take what they can get and have no intention of ever signing a contract or paying you. They'll take advantage of that situation without hesitation. It's essential to assess this on a case-by-case basis. Know your worth and when you're adding value or being taken advantage of. You want to get your foot in the door but don't want to be a doormat.

The key is developing a sense for the difference between strategic generosity and exploitation. Strategic generosity means offering value first but with discernment. It's about providing insights, making introductions, or sharing resources, demonstrating your expertise while building trust. It's not about giving away your core services for free or working endlessly on spec.

I came up through the entertainment industry. I worked at a talent agency where agents would throw phones at us. We're all just people trying to get our work done. I found that I was pissed off from getting mistreated. The main thing I needed to do was not react emotionally. It takes five minutes: write the email, write your thoughts on paper, and say everything you want, but don't hit the send button.

If you had sat on that email until the next day, that issue would have resolved itself—either through a phone call or an in-person meeting—through honest communication, not text communication. Or, by the time you got to that email the next day, it magically resolved itself. This thinning comes with maturity. When you work for somebody else, everything is a high priority. Don't be reactive; be proactive.

This lesson about emotional control relates directly to the effect of generosity. When you're genuinely generous with your network, ideas, and time, you build up what I call "relationship capital." That capital creates a buffer when misunderstandings happen or when someone takes too much. Your generosity has already established enough goodwill that the relationship can withstand occasional tension.

The generosity effect also manifests in how we approach

our work. Everybody wants to work on the big, sexy accounts, but those also come with the most responsibility. The creative who can figure out how to make a campaign for college textbooks or high-interest credit cards sexy is more valuable to me than someone who can make Adobe look sexy. Adobe is already sexy. It's the marketer who can make less flashy subject matter exciting that is harder to find. Suppose you solve the quote-unquote boring problems versus the ones that are easy. That is the key. This approach —finding value and opportunity where others see boring challenges—is another form of generosity. It's generosity toward your clients, offering them your best creative thinking even when the subject matter doesn't immediately inspire. It's generosity toward your team, taking on challenges that might not win awards but build strong foundations for your business.

I've seen the generosity effect play out repeatedly throughout my career. When I approach relationships with a mindset of giving first—whether that's knowledge, connections, or simply time and attention—the returns have been exponential. Not because I expected anything back, but because genuine generosity creates a natural reciprocity. This principle of generosity creating compound returns is substantiated by Dr. Adam Grant's research at Wharton. In his studies of professional success patterns, Grant identified three interaction styles: givers, takers, and matchers. While some givers ended up at the bottom of achievement metrics due to exploitation, the most successful professionals across industries were consistently givers who practiced what Grant calls "otherish giving"—generosity combined with healthy boundaries and strategic focus. Grant's longitudinal studies showed that these strategic givers outperformed their counterparts by generating 50% more valuable professional networks over five-year periods. The generosity effect I've observed throughout my career isn't just anecdotal—it's a documented success pattern across professional domains.

This isn't just my experience. Everyone knows about Steve Jobs's public persona, but his friendship with Oracle's Larry Ellison shows a different side of how deep business relationships can go. These guys weren't just CEO buddies but also neighbors who would take long walks together, discussing everything from business to spirituality. Ellison was even on Apple's board during some crucial years.

Ellison was there when Jobs needed allies during his return to Apple in the late '90s. When Oracle needed to better understand the consumer market, Jobs's insights were invaluable. But they never let business override their friendship. They remained close even when their companies competed in certain areas. They had mutual respect based on actual friendship and innovation.

The lesson isn't just "be nice to your business partners." It's that you have to keep investing in relationships, even when—especially when—things are going well. You can't just coast on past success. The irony is that if they'd maintained the depth of their early relationship—if they'd kept having those honest conversations and maintained a genuine connection—they might have worked through their differences.

Jobs and Ellison demonstrated the generosity effect at its highest level. They gave each other honest feedback, strategic insights, and genuine friendship—not because they calculated the ROI of these exchanges but because they valued the relationship itself. Their mutual generosity created a business relationship that transcended typical corporate boundaries and created lasting value for both men and their companies.

This approach starkly contrasts with the transactional mindset that dominates much of business development today. When you're only generous when you see immediate benefit, people sense that instrumentality. They recognize when they're being "networked" rather than genuinely connected with. The generosity effect only works when it comes from an authentic interest in the other person's success, not just your own.

To make the generosity effect work for you, start small. Look for ways to add unexpected value to every relationship. Make meaningful introductions. Share insights without expecting immediate returns. Celebrate others' successes publicly. These small acts of generosity compound over time, creating a network that generates opportunities you could never create through direct pursuit alone.

The real power of the generosity effect isn't just what it does for your business—it's what it does for your business experience. When you approach your work with a generous contribution rather than an extraction mindset, the entire experience transforms. Work becomes more meaningful, relationships more fulfilling, and success more sustainable. That transformation might be the greatest return on generosity of all.

Fish tacos & canned wine

Here is one example of a client for whom I made a valuable introduction without any thought of what was in it for me. They were launching a canned wine brand in San Diego called Los Cuernos. They were veteran guys in the wine industry since they were both in their twenties. They worked restaurant jobs in LA as high-end waiters, maître d's, and wine sommeliers. I had no way of knowing if the product was good because I'd been sober for ten years, but these two founders were just so enthusiastic about their brand. They were so excited about what they were trying to tackle in the wine industry that all the wine in cans needed improvement. However, wine as a deliverable in a can, especially for the quick service industry and the fast-casual sector, is a great innovation because it allows the customer to have a good experience. It will enable the restaurant to make higher margins and serve their customers faster because they're in a can, and they're not pulling corks and storing bottles of unused wine for long periods.

Since these guys were so enthusiastic when I met them when I got back to the office, I knew that I could be very helpful to them, so I introduced them to the CEO of Wahoo's Fish Tacos. In a short time, we were all headed together to meet with the CEO of Wahoo's Fish Tacos. I still needed to get a contract, but *I hadn't even seen the CEO of Wahoo's for four years. Even getting to go and have face time with him is worth it.* Even if they didn't hire me, they just burned me, took that relationship, and ran with it. The fact that I was getting face time with the CEO of Wahoo's and connecting with those guys was worth the risk of not getting the business.

Because I made the intro and it went well, I signed a decent-sized contract with them, and they fired their CMO. Now we're talking about bringing me on as their new head of marketing. That's an example of how stepping out, being generous, and delivering some added value during the business development process can be highly beneficial. You have to weigh the benefits of that. Introducing the CEO of Wahoo's Fish Tacos, "What's the downside?" There was no downside because, on the one hand, I will ingratiate myself to these founders by introducing them to a critical strategic relationship, and they're going to either take that as a sign of the power of my network and be more interested in hiring me or they would have run with a relationship. Without these guys, I don't have a reason to get in front of the CEO of Wahoo's Fish Tacos. It allowed me to reconnect with Wing, the CEO, and meet with him and the guys in person.

Don't be stingy with introductions if you think it will be helpful to someone. It is a win-win situation. That meeting strengthened my relationship with Wing and again put me at the top of his mental Rolodex. Either way, I win in that situation. In one scenario, I won on both sides of the introduction. In one scenario, I only win half of it, but it's still a win either way. I did something that took me one second: digging up a relationship from my database; somebody I hadn't even talked to in years, dusted them off, and then created mutual value between the three parties. That's one example of something straightforward to do to show value before you "start the work."

Rebel without an expense account

In the startup world, where the David vs. Goliath battle is waged daily, the slingshot isn't just a weapon but a survival tool. As a chief revenue officer who's bootstrapped my way from the ground up, the guy hired on at agencies as employee number three, I've navigated the trenches where big budgets are myths and a polished product is a work in progress. Here's the crux of the hustle: when you're armed with a product that is far from market-leading, your ace is the depth of your relationships.

Think about it–in a landscape saturated with options,

where your prospects could easily opt for a more established, robust offering, why should they choose you? How do you execute at a high level with no budget when you don't even have a great product to sell? The answer lies in the human connection. Those relationships are your currency when capital is scarce. The raw, genuine interactions become your competitive edge, the trust you build when you can't dazzle with flashy marketing campaigns or cut-throat pricing. So, how does a 'rebel' without the cushion of an expense account make a dent? You leverage every conversation, every handshake, and every shared coffee as an opportunity to show value beyond the spreadsheet. You become the CRO who remembers names, listens more than speaks, and turns every potential touchpoint into a memorable encounter.

This is guerrilla warfare in the corporate jungle. It's about outmaneuvering the behemoths not with size but with agility, not with volume but with precision. And when the smoke clears, the relationships you've forged–not the budget you wielded–will stand the test of time. The core idea is to accelerate relationships by going deep quickly, finding common ground, relating on a personal level as much as possible, and purposefully nurturing those intersections between the individual and professional. This means being generous with your time, knowledge, and network without expecting anything immediately in return. The goal is to transform prospects into true partners and lifelong friends, not just close a one-time deal.

Deep persuasion requires patience, emotional investment, and a long-term perspective. It's playing the "long game" in business development. When done right, the depth of the relationships becomes your competitive advantage. Importantly, deep persuasion has to come from a place of sincerity. It's not about faking interest or vulnerability to manipulate others. That "fake vulnerability" backfires and erodes trust. Instead, it's about always trying to add real value for others and letting the strength of the human connection drive the business results organically over time.

Deep persuasion means cultivating business relationships like you would with close friends–through genuine engagement, generosity, and focusing on the long term. It's an approach to sales grounded more in empathy and interdependence than adversarial transactions. Deep persuasion allows mutually beneficial partnerships to emerge naturally from a bedrock of authentic human connection when done well. All the technology and relationship-building strategies don't matter if you can't have honest conversations about value and expectations. I learned this the hard way–trying to be everyone's best friend while dancing around the business conversation. But there's a better way to handle the money talk without breaking the authenticity we've worked so hard to build.

Takeaways from Chapter 7:

- Use AI and automation to create more time for human connection.
- Be transparent about pricing and value early in relationships to build trust.
- Create experiences for key relationships that money can't buy through your network and creativity.
- Focus on long-term relationship value over short-term transactional gains.

PART III
IMPLEMENTATION

CHAPTER 8

Daily practices

I've always been more of a night owl, but I wanted to change that pattern since I typically waste time in the evenings. The turning point came when I attended Jocko Willink's conference, Muster. One of the optional activities was a 4:30 a.m. Navy SEAL workout. Despite my reluctance, I participated and discovered something remarkable.

Getting up that early provided me with uninterrupted time before the world awoke. I experienced San Diego completely differently – deserted streets, quiet contemplation, and most importantly, no interruptions. I had time to exercise, take a sauna, eat breakfast, and mentally prepare before the conference began at 8:30. What I initially thought about productivity became something more valuable: These early hours transformed how I connect with people. Being fully present in conversations becomes difficult when we spend our days reacting to emails, calls, and urgent matters. Our minds race with competing priorities. But in those quiet morning hours, my mind is clear. I can think deeply about the relationships in my life and craft more thoughtful messages.

Now, I naturally wake up between 4 and 6 a.m. without an alarm. The benefits extend beyond just productivity. During those hours, I managed outreach to 500+ contacts programmatically through my CRM, conducted targeted outreach for upcoming conferences, and completed other tasks requiring focus. When my wife wakes up around 6 a.m., I've already accomplished significant work and can spend quality time with her without feeling rushed.

The key insight I've discovered is that changing your schedule drastically works best when paired with activities you genuinely enjoy. Don't just wake up early to check your email. Wake up to do things that energize you. For me, reading and exercise provide that motivation. Working out has become non-negotiable; my brain doesn't function properly in the early mornings without exercise. As Jocko emphasizes, "Discipline equals freedom." While some view freedom as doing whatever you want, true freedom comes from creating a structure that allows you to enter a flow state. The routine tasks happen on autopilot, freeing mental space for deeper learning and meaningful connection.

This isn't about following someone else's perfect morning routine. It's about creating space in your life for authentic connection. How I start my morning sets the tone for my relationships throughout the day. When I'm rushed or reactive, that energy carries into my interactions–I become less patient, less attentive, and less capable of truly listening and connecting. By beginning each day with clarity and intention, I bring a more grounded, focused presence to every conversation. I notice others' needs more readily, ask better questions, and identify opportunities to add value. My morning routine doesn't just enhance my productivity – it serves as the foundation of my relationship-building practice, allowing me to show up as my best self for others consistently.

Setting expectations

One of the worst habits of salespeople is agreeing to anything the client asks for during the discovery call and then chucking that meat over the fence to the account team to execute once they've made a mess. We covered this somewhat when talking about customer support and account teams. Some salespeople will lie about their capabilities and over-promise what they can do within a specific budget. I will gladly admit that I was guilty of that as a younger sales executive. I would go into a conversation and agree to anything that came up during the discovery call. "Oh, yeah, of course, we can tag YouTube videos," before YouTube videos even offered tagging capabilities.

I would agree with all these deliverables, but once we got into the campaign, it turned out that some weren't true. Then, the client team had to deal with it. My deal's already been closed. I'm going to get a commission, and the client's going to have to deal with the things that can't be done, or the account teams will have to deal with the client's disappointment. That was very shortsighted as a rep because it only set me up for a one-time deal. If you lie and or answer questions about technical things that you don't have the expertise to make a judgment call as a salesperson, you're setting yourself up for failure. You might get one deal, but that client's going to be pissed off. When it gets into the implementation phase, and it's too late for them to pull back (maybe not, you could still lose the deal), but say, they've already paid. They're deep into it, and then it comes up that the rep agreed to something that wasn't possible and not profitable for the company, that could not only cost you your reputation but potentially set you up to where you're not going to get repeat business from that client, but it could also open the organization up to liability. It could make the campaign unprofitable, which could damage your job or your reputation as a person within your company.

Salespeople generally get a bad rap for overpromising in meetings and assuming account teams will just figure it out. There's always supposed to be a natural amount of healthy pushback. That's the client's job. I didn't do it out of malice, or think I was lying. I wanted to get stuff done and make a client happy. My perspective is always wanting to please clients and go above and beyond. Make sure that they got the best service and got everything that they were asking for. Our job as salespeople is to be advocates for the clients. We're their internal representative. As the salesperson, you're the one who gets a call if things are going badly, and the client expects you to be their advocate to the delivery team because you're the one who sold them the dream.

The accounts team's job is to be the advocate on behalf of the company. They have to ensure that campaigns get done correctly and on a reasonable timeline. That doesn't overtax or overstress your team to the point where you create bad blood or turnover. Most importantly, they have to run a campaign in a way that's feasible and deliverable, but also make sure that we hit profit margins that are internally benchmarked and make sure that the company is profitable and makes money because none of us are in this for charity work.

If you promise a bunch of additional value, it can come back to bite you. Understanding their context can help you tailor your approach effectively. It's all about aligning with their needs and expectations from the very beginning. Aligning expectations early on ensures that both parties are on the same page, which can significantly improve the engagement's success. It helps build trust and set a clear path forward. Overpromising might secure a quick deal, but underdelivering erodes trust and can damage a business's reputation irreparably.

Consider the countless examples of tech startups that promised revolutionary features to early adopters but failed to deliver due to technical limitations. The short-term gains from initial sales were quickly overshadowed by public disappointment, leading to a significant drop in user trust and market share. Contrast this with companies known for their stringent adherence to ethical sales practices, which report higher customer retention rates and brand loyalty. As sales professionals, our duty extends far beyond closing deals. We are the architects of our clients' trust and the caretakers of our firm's reputation. Each interaction is an opportunity to demonstrate our integrity and foster a relationship beyond mere financial transactions. We can transform short-term interactions into long-lasting partnerships by embracing the art of silence, asking the right questions, and setting honest expectations. This commitment to ethical selling and client advocacy sets us apart in a competitive market and builds a foundation for enduring success.

Never turn down a meeting

I have a standing principle: I will meet with anybody who contacts me. I don't care if they're an insurance broker or a financial planner. If somebody is willing to meet with me in person and do it on my terms based on my schedule, if they're eager to go to the coffee shop that's eight minutes down the road from my house, I will meet with them, even if they're just looking for an intro for a job. I recently met with Norma, a San Diego transplant and very successful media seller who has worked at great companies throughout her life. However, she found herself in San Diego, a non-media market, facing ageism in the industry. She'd been unemployed for nine months and was looking for new opportunities. She got on my radar through local pickleball marketing meetups I'd started hosting.

I met with Norma for coffee, and she explained her situation and story. The reality is that I had nothing to gain from helping her except being generous and putting good energy out there. When I got home from our coffee meeting, she sent the follow-up email with her cover letter and the position she was interested in at Power Digital Marketing. I searched my LinkedIn network and discovered I was connected with the chairman and founder. Though I hadn't spent much time getting to know this person and had never met him outside of LinkedIn, I grabbed his email and made an introduction. He was excited to meet a qualified prospect from somebody he was at least aware of, and he forwarded her information to HR.

This reinforces that you must be somewhat guarded with your calendar–you can't spend 24 hours a day life-coaching people who need something from you. But my perspective is that this person had engaged, reached out, was willing to negotiate a meeting on my terms, was willing to drive from Point Loma to North County San Diego (30 minutes), and was willing to buy me coffee, which is generous and unexpected. She was willing to be vulnerable about where she was in her career and life, and just asked for a connection.

What did that take me? A short drive down the hill and an hour-long meeting to get to know this woman. I genuinely enjoy hearing people's stories. It was fun to understand how she ended up in San Diego and what she was dealing with. If Norma goes to work for that agency, she'll never forget how she ended up working there, and it will put me on the founder's radar. The next time I ask him for a meeting or favor, my currency will have gone up with him from helping secure a good employee. Technology can help manage relationships at our going-deep framework's contact and context levels. Still, the deeper connection and community stages require genuine human engagement that no algorithm can replace.

You never know who somebody else might know or the potential next level of introduction. Many try to be too judicious by only meeting with whoever they consider mission-critical deal prospects or people they think they can do business with directly. However, you must consider an indirect secondary network when meeting and building relationships. It's the idea that the bigger your network is, the more feelers you have out in the world of people who might be able to introduce you to the right person, even if they're not the right person themselves, and that's also how you recruit super connectors to your network.

While I believe in the value of unexpected connections, 'never turn down a meeting' is more philosophy than a literal rule. I approach unexpected meeting requests with an open mind rather than immediate skepticism. That doesn't mean saying yes to every coffee invitation at the expense of existing commitments or personal well-being. Instead, I follow a flexible triage approach: If someone reaches out thoughtfully and I have genuine capacity, I'll typically say yes. If my schedule is full but the person shows real effort in their outreach, I might suggest a brief call instead of coffee or schedule something several weeks out. And if the request feels purely transactional or poorly considered, I'll politely decline or redirect. The principle isn't about saying yes to everything—it's about remaining open to serendipity while respecting your existing commitments. The relationships that matter most—both established and potential—deserve your thoughtful consideration rather than automatic rejection or acceptance.

Generally, when starting at a new position, I will leverage my networks to build relationships more quickly versus going out cold to prospect. For instance, one of the things that I've mentioned already is that I like to use Sigma Chi as a common denominator or a place to start when building out a new network for a new ideal customer profile, because that gives me some degree of relevance when I'm reaching out to people. Not everybody cares much about Sigma Chi after college, but it's at least a shared experience I had with this person. They feel some sort of—maybe not obligation, but at least hopefully enough positive memories or positive association that they might say, "Okay, well, this guy is associated with this common network that I'm a part of, so I'll at least give him an opportunity, and I tend to do the same thing in the other direction."

Similarly, if any Sigma Chi reaches out to me, I'll at least read the email and do my best to be helpful. Most likely, I'll take a meeting. It may not fit in as a tier-one priority in my calendar, but if I have open space, I'll take that meeting and see if I can be helpful. It's an unspoken rule, at least with some who consider that a high degree of currency. When working at Channel Factory, I reached out to prospects who were Sigma Chis and Sigma Chis in general, especially when traveling. Sometimes, I would have only one meeting on the calendar. If I had been in a separate city for some time, there would have been a limited window to meet new people from that city in person.

I once had a core meeting in Chicago, but then I filled it up with additional prospect meetings and even some general networking meetings with Sigma Chi. I met with a guy who had nothing to do with marketing or advertising—he was just a Sigma Chi, so it was just a general networking meeting. We got together for coffee, talked about our college experiences, and got to know each other. It turned out that his brother-in-law was the Chief Communications Officer of the Discovery Channel, a significant C-suite position at a massive TV network out in Washington, DC. And this is a family relative of this person.

I told him that if he were willing to make an introduction, I would bring him on part-time as a consultant and compensate him if we did any business with him. So I did that. I brought him on as a consultant just for this one relationship. I flew him out to DC. We both went together for the meeting because if I have this guy under my corporate umbrella as an employee, how much more likely is his brother-in-law willing to try and do something if his brother will benefit from it? You can view that as nepotism or negative in some way, but people like to do business with people they enjoy being around.

His brother-in-law, the Chief Communications Officer, got the entire media team into a room for us, probably ten people from the Discovery Channel, all the relevant departments, all the relevant shows, all the relevant divisions, and we were able to do a dog and pony show for the entire room. We may have only gotten one deal directly with them, but we then got an introduction to their media agency, OMD, and continued to get RFPs from OMD from that point forward. That was when a significant door opened, and I could have considered that initial meeting a waste of time–a meeting with a stranger who had nothing to do with my industry. But you just never know who other people know.

Another component is trying to find your super connectors and your referral sources. There's another guy here in San Diego named John Fraser. He's a venture capitalist investor type, and he was introduced to me through a media agency here in San Diego during COVID-19. I got together with him for coffee, and he represented an influencer with 22 million followers. We hired him and brought him into our agency to do business development and build our talent department. Even though John's background wasn't in my industry, he was super relevant to meet and get to know. Even though we were no longer colleagues working together officially, he continued to be one of my most significant sources of referrals for my new agency and the stuff that I'm doing today. He introduced me to somebody almost once or twice a week.

Reading the room

I had two meetings the same week that showed that everyone is different, and you can't force going deep on a personal level. The first meeting that week was with a VP of marketing at a major tech company. I noticed that his office had no personal photos, no decorations—just awards and industry recognition. When I tried to make small talk about his weekend, he gave short, polite answers and quickly steered us back to business. Every attempt to connect personally was met with professional courtesy but clear boundaries. Some people might see this as a failed attempt at relationship building, but I saw it as valuable information. This person told me exactly how they wanted to interact—professionally, efficiently, and focused on results.

The next day, I met with a Chief Brand Officer who had her kids' artwork all over her walls and immediately told me about the painting class she'd taken over the weekend. Her eyes lit up when I shared that I'd considered taking art classes with my daughter. We spent the first twenty minutes of our meeting talking about parenting and creativity before naturally transitioning to business. The conversation flowed between personal and professional topics throughout our meeting.

SIGNS SOMEONE'S Open to Going Deeper:

- They volunteer personal information unprompted
- Their body language is open and engaged
- They ask you personal questions in return
- They take time to elaborate on their answers
- They share challenges or vulnerabilities
- They show genuine curiosity about your perspective

SIGNS TO KEEP THINGS PROFESSIONAL:

- They consistently redirect to business topics
- Their answers are brief and strictly professional
- They maintain formal body language
- They check their watch or phone frequently
- They don't reciprocate personal sharing

- They use institutional "we" language instead of "I"

THE KEY IS RESPECTING where people are at. Not everyone wants or needs a deep relationship, and that's okay. Some of my most successful long-term business relationships started very professionally and only gradually deepened over years of consistent interaction. One powerful example of quiet influence in action is the leadership style of former Costco CEO Jim Sinegal. Sinegal was known for his humble, understated approach. He didn't seek the spotlight but focused on building deep, authentic relationships with his employees, suppliers, and customers. Under his leadership, Costco became known for its strong company culture and loyal customer base, not through flashy marketing campaigns but through a quiet commitment to doing right by all stakeholders. Sinegal demonstrated that lasting influence often comes not from being the loudest voice in the room but from consistently showing up with integrity and genuine care for others. But here's the reality nobody likes to discuss: Relationships still hit rough patches even when you do everything right. The depth of your relationships isn't tested when everything's going great–it's tested when things go sideways.

Networking events

You have to get out there and try to find other super connectors in your community, even if they are in a different industry. Just meet and connect with as many people as possible. Think about other professional services and people who have to network for a living. For instance, financial advisors, people who sell insurance, real estate agents, CPAs, business consultants, marketing people, etc. I've found many of these types of people lately in leads meetings. If you go online and search for networking events in your area, you'll find something happening all the time. I see 10 to 20 events around San Diego daily, likely similar in every major city.

These are great opportunities to connect with other like-minded super connectors because they attend these meetings to build a referral partner network. Go into it with an open mind and understand that you'll probably get pitched here and there for real estate services, life insurance, or whatever. Still, if you are earnest and helpful and potentially introduce those people to the types of folks they want to meet, that reciprocity will return to you tenfold.

The central concept here is that you never know where or how you'll make a connection that will alter the course of your life. If you have white space in your calendar, you might as well fill it out. Meeting people in person is more important, especially for business development people. You can develop stronger relationships in person by building relationships and cultivating a referral network rather than sitting in front of your computer. You'll start creating super referral sources that send you more inbound leads.

People who seem entirely irrelevant to your day-to-day life may know people who are highly relevant to your day-to-day life. Suppose you have white space in your calendar, somebody reaches out to you, or you're trying to build your network. In that case, taking those meetings to see if you can make a relationship is always advantageous. It's harder to do over Zoom these days. Getting out there and getting into situations like networking events or leading groups is better for fostering genuine human connections. These groups have a format particular to the idea that everybody is getting to know each of the members, understanding what they do and their business models, and being intentional about trying to find folks that might be interesting for them to meet. As you begin to recruit this network of super connectors and like-minded people who are out doing the same thing, within weeks, you could have 10 or 20 people who have you top of mind. Then, you build a referral engine that sends you more business than you can handle.

A referral from a trustworthy source is always 1,000 times more relevant because the chances are they've been qualified. They need precisely what you do, or your super connector partner, your referral network, would not have even considered you. Based on their credibility, they're endorsing you by introducing you, so there's already a level of vetting and qualification.

You can go out there and build relationships with as many like-minded people as possible who are in the business of meeting other people. In that case, you can supercharge your network and create a potent referral source. The power of networking cannot be overstated when it comes to growing your business and unlocking new opportunities. By adopting a mindset of never turning down a meeting and actively seeking out like-minded, well-connected individuals, you can significantly expand your reach and tap into a vast network of potential referral sources. Remember, you never know who someone might know or how a seemingly irrelevant connection could lead to a game-changing opportunity. By investing time in building genuine relationships, attending networking events, and cultivating a network of super connectors, you can create a powerful referral engine that consistently sends high-quality leads your way.

I shared earlier about the outreach process of using both

a sniper rifle and the elephant gun–getting mass outreach done on the early side through 500 people daily through CRM. Another 20 people a day through Reply.io, and then everything else is a sniper rifle, one-to-one. A great way to start one-to-one outreach is based around events and conferences. I'll go on Google and see if there are any marketing conferences. If you type in "marketing conference," it'll look at your IP address and serve results in your geographic region. For me, it's stuff in San Diego, Palm Springs, and Los Angeles. I'll first look and see if there are any local events I can reach out to people around, because then I'll have the chance to meet them in person. Then, I'll look at events that I put in my calendar–events that are taking place in other cities. Each March, there is AdAge, Gen. Z. Summit in New York, the AMA Awards, a direct-to-consumer conference in Austin, South by Southwest in Austin, and the B2B Expo in Miami. I'm not at these events, and I'm not planning to go, but I'm doing outreach as if I were at all of them. The idea is that if I do get a significant meeting, I would probably hop on a plane and take that meeting.

Most of the time, if you reach out one-on-one to people speaking on a panel or keynote, people will just reply to the email with a version of, "Oh, thanks for reaching out. Let's do a call afterward. I don't have time right now." It can be a great way to touch base with someone and start a conversation. Often, people are not that interested when you're doing just generic outreach. They feel a low sense of urgency because if I'm reaching out and saying I could meet with you any time, then there's no set sense of urgency. But suppose I'm contacting you about a conference you're excited about and attending in person. In that case, there's this base level of credibility that we either got invited to speak or we're there because we paid a few bucks to attend the conference, and that's also creating urgency because it's around a compressed window of time. If I'm reaching out and saying, "Hey, let's meet at this conference," that conference is only going on for 1, 2, 3, maybe ten days for something like South by Southwest, that drags on. That false sense of scarcity, of having a limited window to meet with someone, allows people to say, *Okay, I'll prioritize this because I've only got 1 or 2 days to make this meeting happen*, and there's some level of qualification because we're both in the right place at the right time.

I love doing outreach around events, even if I do not intend to attend the event. The one asterisk that I'll put on this strategy is that you can piss off the event planner or whoever is putting on the conference. MediaPost Communications banned me from all meetings for this tactic. They won't let me come to their events, and the reality is, if I even showed up and went on the property where one of their events is being held, I would get escorted off the property. You can ruffle the feathers of the meeting planner or conference planner. But I've only ever had that happen once. Most people don't care if you're reaching out to people like that (even if you don't have a ticket).

The balancing act

When I first started interviewing CROs and CMOs of Fortune 500 companies for my podcast, one of the main things that I wanted to learn from them was how they managed to be good parents and good friends. How are they able to be good for their communities? How do they manage well-rounded lives as high-level business development people? I have found the sad reality is that we're terrible at it.

I focus most of my day on talking to strangers and trying to implement the principles that we're talking about. I want to go deep and get to know them better, and have the business be a by-product of that relationship. I don't do it to be manipulative. One of my favorite things is hearing people's stories. Where did they grow up? How many kids do they have? What are they interested in? What makes them tick? I never really understand my value proposition during an initial business meeting or call. I always focus on who they are and their story. It's a lot more interesting to learn about who somebody is and their backstory than to go through a deck. The business can get figured out if we like each other as people. Most importantly, client relationships involve spending a lot of time with people, whether in person or over the phone. I must like them; they must like me if they want to trust me. I spend most of my time building relationships over product fit.

As I already mentioned, my co-author, Nate Pettijohn, and I met over 15 years ago in the context of business while I was building up a network of people in the entertainment industry who were Sigma Chis, so we could network and build relationships with each other and share deal flow. Today, we are still close friends. We still do business together (proven by his helping me create this book). This is the case for most of my best friends, and I have a lot of friends. I certainly don't want to come across as complaining about a lack of relationships, but my best friends are people I've known professionally first. What happens for salespeople is that we spend so much time pouring into the relationship-building process of meeting strangers and trying to get them to like and trust us that by the time we finish our day, we're entirely out of gas. We only have enough energy left for our spouses and kids, and not as much for "friends," People we will spend time with outside of a professional relationship.

Nate and I have mutual friends, like Nic de Castro and Matt Ward. Those were the guys who were my competitors when we first interacted. They were my sworn enemies in the marketplace when I led sales at Channel Factory. I went up against them all the time. I occasionally had to trash-talk them and throw them under the bus for things they were doing, and they would do the same thing to me. I got to know these guys because we were always at the same conferences, and we discovered that we had mutual interests (including a love for cigars). Then that community became bigger; it became this whole network effect where we're now all close friends. But at the start, we were sworn competitors in the professional world.

There have been moments when I was so focused on the external relationship that I took my family for granted. When my first daughter was born, she was born a week "late." So, even though I took two weeks off work because she was born a week late, I was on a plane within a week. When my second daughter was born, I returned to work the next day. If somebody said, "Dylan, get on a plane," I would get on a plane. I would go anywhere in the world, anytime, for a client. That was just how I operated. I ended up traveling most of the time at the expense of my family.

Love it or hate it, the blessing of COVID-19 is that it completely reoriented the idea to "you don't have to get on a plane." Nowadays, I rarely get on a plane. Last year, I took a single business trip to Austin. All of my prospecting and meetings happen in Southern California. I just wait. I troll every conference in Southern California and wait for people to go to LA. I am waiting for them to come to San Diego. I wait for the meetings to come to me, and if those things don't happen, we just get on a call. I am rarely willing to leave town nowadays unless there is an opportunity to bring my family with me. If they can travel with me, I'm adding a vacation and bringing my family along. Sadly, it had to be something like COVID-19 that reoriented many businesspeople's brains into the idea that we *don't have to live like that as business development people. We cannot jump on a plane every time a client rings a bell.*

Now, I'm a present dad. I've invested in my kids. What's been exciting about spending more time at home is my wife; we've got two kids, 8 and 10, and we have a one-year-old, and my wife just decided to get back into the workforce. We're busier than ever, but she still feels like she can return to the workforce because I'm a co-parent now, probably for the first time in my life. I'm willing to change diapers and stay home with the kids so she can go out, have a business meeting, or do something to satisfy her professional ambitions. We also work together now in her small agency. She's already generated enough income to be comparable to mine. Just a little bit of empowering her to focus again on what made her flourish in her early career has been a huge financial boon for our family.

Before COVID-19, I would travel 50% of the time. I would jump on a plane to Pittsburgh if a client said to go or do a 13-day business trip to New York, Washington, DC, Boston, and Atlanta. It caused friction in my life, kept me away from my kids, and caused my wife to raise them by herself at different times. Now, I get sad when I leave my family. I focus on what I can get done in San Diego. Are there networking events I can organize for myself? Are there conferences coming to San Diego? How can I start with my backyard and return home to my family when I'm done working? If nothing's happening in San Diego, I look at what's happening in Irvine, Palm Springs, Orange County, LA, and Santa Barbara–places I could drive to and still come home. The next level out is Phoenix, Las Vegas, and San Francisco. If I can't bring my family with me or it's not somewhere I can drive, I'm probably not doing it anymore. I bring my family to conferences, and they get to hang out at the pool and hotel. I see them at the end of the night. I might not spend much time with them, but we usually add two to three days of family time at the end of the trip.

The hardest part of building deep relationships in business isn't finding time or saying the right things–it's staying true to those relationships when business pressures push you to do otherwise. I've faced this countless times, particularly during my years at Channel Factory when quarterly targets loomed and investor expectations were high. There was a period when I was pushing myself and my team to hit aggressive growth targets. I had relationships with CMOs at several major brands who trusted me and with whom I'd built genuine connections over the years. The easy path would have been to leverage those relationships, push for more significant contracts, ask for introductions to their networks, and essentially cash in on the trust we'd built.

But that's precisely when you have to remember why you built those relationships in the first place. It wasn't to hit a quarterly number. It wasn't to impress investors. It was because a genuine human connection makes both business and life more meaningful. I've watched other executives handle this differently. They build relationships until they need something, and then they strip-mine those relationships for whatever value they can extract. It might work in the short term, but it creates a wake of burned bridges and damaged trust. I've learned to resist that pressure and protect relationships' authenticity, even when it means missing a business goal.

This isn't just idealism–it's practical. The depth of your relationships is what carries you through tough times. When my business hit rough patches, it wasn't the transactional relationships that helped me weather the storm. I built genuine connections with those who knew me as more than just a vendor or partner. The reality is that deep relationships and business success aren't at odds. They're complementary; you have to be willing to prioritize the relationship over the immediate business opportunity. Sometimes, that means turning down deals that would compromise trust. Sometimes, it means being honest when telling people what they want to hear would be easier. It always means remembering that authentic connection is the foundation on which everything else is built.

Takeaways from Chapter 8:

- Establish morning routines that create mental space for relationship-building activities.
- Set clear expectations with clients and colleagues to prevent relationship damage from misunderstandings.
- Consider meeting with everyone who reaches out thoughtfully, as unexpected connections often yield surprising value.
- Learn to "read the room" and adjust your approach based on how others prefer to connect.

CHAPTER 9

When trust breaks

The deeper your relationships go in business, the more it hurts when things go wrong. I've learned this lesson repeatedly, but never more painfully than once when we had to tell a major client we couldn't deliver what we'd promised. We'd committed to a complex influencer campaign involving multiple high-profile creators. Everything looked solid on paper. The client trusted us based on years of successful projects. Then, three days before the launch, two key influencers pulled out. Not just any influencers, but the ones upon which the entire campaign was built. We had backup plans for most scenarios, but not this one. Not at this scale.

I had two choices: I could try to patch things together with replacement influencers or be completely honest about the situation. The first option might have saved the campaign in the short term, but it meant delivering something far below what we'd promised. The second option meant admitting failure and potentially losing a major client. I chose honesty. I called the client personally, but there was no email or Zoom; it was just a direct phone call. I explained exactly what had happened, acknowledged where we'd failed in our contingency planning, and offered to refund their investment plus cover their internal costs. I expected anger. Instead, I got something that taught me everything about real relationship recovery.

The client said, "I appreciate you calling me directly about this. Most people would have tried to cover it up or make excuses. Let's figure out how to make this right together." That moment crystallized something I'd felt but hadn't fully understood: Recovery isn't about fixing a specific problem in deep relationships. It's about demonstrating that you value the relationship more than your ego or short-term interests.

The relationship between Phil Knight and Jeff Johnson is one of those stories that hits close to home because it shows how even the most profound business relationships can fracture–and sometimes heal in unexpected ways. Johnson was Nike's first-ever employee. He wasn't just any employee; he was the guy who came up with the name "Nike." He opened their first retail store. He was so passionate about the business that he'd write Knight these incredibly detailed, multi-page letters about everything from shoe design to customer feedback. Despite being crucial to Nike's early success, Johnson and Knight had a falling out in 1971. They were growing fast, and Knight wanted to systematize everything. Johnson was more of an entrepreneur and wanted to do things his way. It got to the point where they couldn't even be in the same room. Johnson left the company he helped build. I've seen this kind of thing happen too often in my career–relationships that seemed unbreakable somehow break. Usually, things that, in hindsight, could have been worked through if both parties had stepped back and remembered what made their partnership valuable in the first place.

What's fascinating about the Knight-Johnson story is what happened next. They didn't speak for years. But slowly, over time, something shifted. Knight recognized that some of Johnson's "crazy" ideas had been right. Johnson gained perspective on why Knight had pushed for more structure. When they finally reconnected years later, it wasn't about who had been right or wrong. It was about acknowledging that they'd tried to do what they thought was best for the company. Today, Nike's most advanced research lab is named after Jeff Johnson. A relationship that seemed permanently broken not only healed but became part of the company's legacy.

Sometimes, what feels like an irreparable break is just a necessary pause. Both parties need time to grow, to gain perspective, and to understand what the relationship was really about in the first place. The key is to leave the door open and not let pride or hurt feelings turn a temporary break into a permanent one. I've had my version of this story with certain clients and partners. Times when things got heated, when it seemed like there was no way forward. But I've learned to ask myself: am I trying to win an argument, or am I trying to preserve a relationship that could be valuable for years to come? Sometimes, taking a step back and giving things time to cool off can make all the difference. Crisis moments test whether you've truly gone deep or merely simulated depth. In authentic, deep relationships, the mutual value creation and long-term orientation elements create resilience that can withstand temporary setbacks.

The layoff test

Sometimes, relationship setbacks come from circumstances beyond your control. I've been through multiple rounds of layoffs and acquisitions, both as the person leaving and staying. These transitions test the depth of your business relationships like nothing else. When I left my one particular role, I had dozens of client relationships I'd built over the years. The easy path was to take those relationships with me to my next venture. Many people do precisely that–they treat client relationships as portable assets. But that approach fundamentally misunderstands what deep relationships are about. Instead, I spent my last weeks there ensuring each client had a solid transition plan. I introduced them to their new contact points, shared detailed context about their business needs, and clarified that I trusted my former colleagues to care for them. Some clients later chose to work with me in my new role, but that wasn't the goal. The goal was to honor the relationships themselves, regardless of where they led.

Here's another example with Adobe. Even though they're no longer clients of mine, I still consider them close friends and valuable professional relationships. I've been working hard for three months with my new client, Lost In, having good conversations and RFPs, but all the effort has been cold because I don't have a deep Rolodex in the travel industry. My Adobe contact, Jayson, recently called out of the blue, saying, "I know you're working with Lost In. A guy I used to work with, Damian, just became the Chief Marketing Officer of Big Bear, and he's looking for opportunities." He connected us over text, and within 30 minutes, Damian invited me to Big Bear, offering three nights in an

Airbnb, free lift tickets to Snow Summit, and $150 in food vouchers so we could meet and discuss ways to partner.

I had my first in-person pitch in an office with a team post-COVID-19, which was a fantastic experience. They became my first client at Lost In. While I spent three months pounding the pavement trying to build warm relationships and attending conferences, this connection through someone I've stayed current with accelerated everything, even though they're not my client anymore. We still go on vacation together and hang out, and I went with him to shoot content for a cigar company in the Dominican Republic just to hang out together.

Because I'm top of mind for him, when he saw an opportunity to refer me, it accelerated quickly and leapfrogged all other deals in my pipeline. It also made me aware of a target I would never have considered. As a salesperson, I'm going after the biggest spenders in tourism—Big Bear isn't even on the top 100 list. Because of the relationship and their priorities, it quickly became a substantial account. Not only that, but Damian has also become one of my favorite new people. We're developing a medical tourism concept around his husband, who is taking people to South America to explore plant-based medicine. We're building an even deeper relationship because I'm helping with their passion project outside the Big Bear tourism work. I've introduced him to brand storytelling people, and they might do a conference there. Keep adding value, adding value, adding value, and accelerating the speed of that relationship. Now he's inviting me to Washington, D.C., to meet Robert Kennedy Jr. and his team because he's neighbors with them.

All these doors opened because of a warm introduction. If I had been callous and cut ties with my Adobe clients after they fired us, I could have harbored ill will or had a grudge. Losing that business was hugely impactful–I got laid off. But because I didn't take it personally and continued building that relationship, not only because I love spending time with Jayson as a person, but because I appreciate him and want to keep that door open, it led to new opportunities. It didn't necessarily mean returning to Adobe, but he opened another substantial door for my latest ventures.

When you're building deep relationships in business, there's always this tension between collaboration and competition. Nobody understood this better than Mary Kay Ash. Here's a woman who built a billion-dollar empire by doing something that most people would consider crazy: She actively encouraged top salespeople to help their potential competitors succeed. This hits home for me because we're always walking that line in the media and influencer space. There's only so much of a brand budget, and viewing every other agency or sales rep as a competitor can be tempting. But Mary Kay had this insight that completely flipped that mindset.

She created a concept called "dual marketing," where sales directors would actively train and mentor other people who could technically become their competition. On paper, this makes no sense. Why would you train someone who might take business away from you? But here's what she understood: real success comes from expanding the pie, not just fighting over the same slice. I saw this play out in my career while working at Channel Factory. Some of my biggest competitors—Nic de Castro and Matt Ward—became close friends (to both Nate and me). We'd see each other at conferences, start hanging out, and discover we loved cigars. Now, these guys, whom I used to have to trash-talk to win deals, are some of my closest confidants. We share insights, help each other out, and make each other better.

Mary Kay took this even further. She instituted this rule that if one of your team members moved up to become a sales director, you couldn't be resentful–you had to celebrate it. She'd have people stand up and applaud when someone who used to work under them became their peer. Think about how radical that is in business culture. Most people get defensive when their subordinates rise. When you approach competition this way, you create a network of people who are invested in each other's success. Mary Kay used to say, "There's enough business for everyone." When I first heard that, it was just a lovely saying. But the older I get, the more I realize it's a profound business strategy.

Instead of viewing other sales leaders or agencies as competition, I look for ways to help each other grow. Sometimes, that means sharing resources; sometimes, it means making introductions; and sometimes, it just means being genuinely happy when they succeed. It's counterintuitive, but the more I help potential competitors, the more opportunities come my way. The real test of this approach comes during tough times, when budgets are tight or the market is down. That's when most people retreat into competition mode. But if you've built genuine relationships with your so-called competitors, those relationships often become your safety net. They're the ones who send you referrals when they're not the right fit for a client or who help you spot opportunities you might have missed.

Cross-cultural dimensions

"But Dylan, this approach might work in American business culture, but what about when dealing internationally?" This is an objection I've heard, and it highlights an important consideration.

Different cultures have varying norms around relationship building, self-disclosure, and business boundaries. In some cultures, business discussions happen only after extensive personal relationship building. In others, mixing personal and professional is seen as inappropriate. Some cultures value direct communication; others prioritize harmony and indirect messaging. When I worked with Chinese clients at Channel Factory, I had to adjust my approach significantly. They expected professional competence and reliability to be established first, with personal relationship elements developing gradually. My usual pattern of asking personal questions early and suggesting informal social activities initially created discomfort.

I adjusted by focusing our early interactions on business objectives, technical capabilities, and strategic alignment. Only after establishing this foundation did I gradually introduce more personal elements—and even in more structured settings than I would typically choose with American clients. What I discovered wasn't that I needed to become a different person—just that I needed to express my authentic interest in relationship-building through different patterns and timing. The core principle of genuine curiosity and interest remained the same, but the expression became culturally appropriate.

Trust signals vary dramatically across cultural contexts. I learned that taking time for relationship development was a trust signal when working with Middle Eastern clients. What might feel like unnecessary delays to an American businessperson—multiple meetings with substantial non-business discussion before getting to terms—was essential relationship foundation-building. With European clients, particularly in Germany and Scandinavia, I've found that respecting personal boundaries while engaging deeply on intellectual and strategic levels creates the strongest connections. Attempting to rush personal familiarity often backfires. Trust develops through consistent delivery, intellectual respect, and appropriate gradual disclosure.

Research on gender and leadership by scholars like Deborah Tannen and Alice Eagly has documented how the dynamics of professional relationships are influenced by gender. Women in business often navigate different expectations around relationship-building than their male counterparts. Studies have shown that women in leadership positions frequently face what researchers call the "double bind"—behaviors that might be perceived as appropriately assertive by men and may be interpreted as aggressive when displayed by women. Similarly, vulnerability that might be seen as authentic coming from men may be perceived as weakness when shown by women. This creates additional complexities for women implementing the "going deep" approach. Women across many cultures report developing strategic approaches to professional vulnerability, often demonstrating competence before revealing more personal dimensions of themselves.

Research by the Pew Research Center and other organizations studying workplace dynamics has documented how relationship-building varies significantly across generations. Younger professionals often bring different expectations to business relationships than their older colleagues. Studies show that Gen Z and younger Millennials typically expect more authenticity and alignment between personal and professional values in workplace relationships. They're also more comfortable maintaining meaningful connections through digital channels than previous generations. This generational perspective challenges traditional relationship-building approaches that prioritize formal, in-person interaction. While face-to-face communication still creates the strongest connections, according to relationship science, younger professionals have developed sophisticated ways to signal trust and build depth through digital communication.

The core elements of going deep—authentic connection, appropriate vulnerability, long-term orientation, mutual value creation, and intentional depth—remain consistent across cultures. What changes is how these elements are expressed, their timing, and their relative emphasis. Business relationships operate within cultural contexts, but they ultimately happen between individuals. Cross-cultural research consistently shows that demonstrating genuine respect and interest transcends cultural boundaries. A more profound connection becomes possible when people sense that you genuinely value their perspective, not despite cultural differences but inclusive of them.

Rather than going in with predetermined ideas about how relationship-building "should" work, I try to understand how it functions in that specific context. This doesn't mean abandoning my fundamental approach to going deep. The core elements—authentic connection, appropriate vulnerability, long-term orientation, mutual value creation, and intentional depth—remain consistent. What changes is the expression, timing, and emphasis of these elements. Across all cultural differences, I've found one universal truth: genuine respect transcends boundaries. A deeper connection becomes possible when people sense that you value their perspective and approach, not despite cultural differences but including them.

When to let go

Not every relationship can or should be saved. This is one of the hardest lessons I've had to learn. Sometimes, despite your best efforts and genuine intentions, a relationship has run its course. The trick is recognizing the difference between a relationship that needs work and one that needs to end. I had a long-term client relationship that looked perfect on paper. The numbers were good, and the feedback was positive, but something felt off. Every interaction required enormous energy. Every decision involved intense negotiation. We were going through the motions of a deep relationship without the underlying trust and mutual understanding that make deep relationships valuable.

It took me too long to realize that I was preventing both parties from finding better partnerships by trying to force this relationship to work. Sometimes, the most decisive move you can make for a relationship is recognizing when to let it go. That doesn't mean burning bridges. It means having the courage to say, "I don't think we're the best fit for each other anymore." It means being willing to help transition to a new partner. It means maintaining respect and professionalism even as you create distance. But how do you know when a relationship has crossed that point of no return versus when it's just going through a rough patch that could strengthen your connection in the long run? I've developed a few reliable indicators to help make this crucial distinction over the years.

Assess the pattern, not just the incident. Every relationship hits bumps—a miscommunication, a missed deadline, a disagreement about approach. What matters isn't that these things happen but the pattern around them. As you learn each other's working styles, these incidents become less frequent in salvageable relationships. You develop systems to prevent the same problems from recurring. If you're seeing the same conflicts repeatedly despite genuine efforts to address the underlying issues, that's a warning sign. Then, evaluate the energy exchange. Even during challenging periods, healthy relationships have a relatively balanced energy exchange. You might invest heavily during certain phases, but it doesn't consistently feel like you're carrying the entire weight of the relationship. When I look back at relationships I should have ended sooner, the common thread was constant depletion—I'd leave every interaction feeling drained rather than energized or at least neutral. If this imbalance persists for months without improvement, it's usually a sign that the relationship structure isn't working.

Every relationship experiences trust challenges, but there's a difference between trust that's been damaged by specific actions and can be rebuilt versus trust that was never properly established. I've successfully repaired relationships where trust was broken by a clear mistake that was acknowledged and addressed. I've never been able to fix relationships where, despite surface cordiality, there was a fundamental lack of trust in each other's intentions. When someone consistently assumes the worst about your motives, despite evidence to the contrary, that's extremely difficult to overcome.

Be honest about alignment. Some relationships struggle not because either party is doing anything wrong but because their fundamental approaches, values, or objectives have diverged too far. I had a client relationship that started strong when both our companies were startups with similar cultures and goals. As they grew into a large corporation with multiple layers of approval and risk-aversion, while we remained entrepreneurial and fast-moving, the friction became constant. Neither of us was wrong—we had simply evolved in different directions that no longer complemented each other. When you spot these indicators, it doesn't mean you should immediately end the relationship. Instead, I recommend one explicit conversation where you directly address the pattern you're seeing and ask if they perceive it the same way. Sometimes, this conversation can be the turning point that saves the relationship. Other times, it confirms that both parties have been feeling the strain and creates space for an amicable conclusion.

Remember that ending a relationship well doesn't mean it failed. Some of my most positive business outcomes have come from having the courage to acknowledge when a relationship had served its purpose for both parties and then helping each other transition to more fitting partnerships. Years later, this approach resulted in referrals and reconnections under different circumstances where we were better aligned.

The interesting thing about relationship recovery is that, often, the most challenging moments, the failures, the transitions, the honest conversations about things not working, all become the foundation for even stronger connections. It's like what happens when you break a bone: if it heals properly, that spot can become stronger than it was before. I've had relationships that seemed permanently damaged but came back stronger years later, precisely because we handled the difficult moment with honesty and respect. I've had clients who left during tough times return specifically because they remembered how we handled their departure.

The key is remembering that every interaction, even the difficult ones, perhaps especially the difficult ones, is part of the longer story of your relationship. Focusing on immediate damage control in a crisis or failure is easy. But if you've built real depth in your relationships and invested in genuine trust and understanding, serious setbacks become opportunities to demonstrate what those relationships mean. This isn't about having a perfect record. It's about having the courage to be imperfect, admit mistakes quickly, and prioritize long-term trust over short-term success. Ultimately, how you handle failure says more about the depth of your relationships than how you handle success.

<u>Takeaways from Chapter 9:</u>

- Handle relationship setbacks directly and honestly rather than avoiding difficult conversations.
- Focus on relationship preservation over being right when conflicts arise.
- Apply the "layoff test" to your relationships - maintain connections even when formal business relationships end.
- Recognize when relationships have run their course and gracefully transition to new partnerships.

10

CHAPTER 10

Building your legacy

You might wonder why I'm ending this book by talking about legacy. Isn't that something you worry about at the end of your career? But here's what I've learned: The legacy you build isn't just about what you leave behind–it's about how you show up every day. The relationships you make, the trust you earn, the value you create for others–that's your real legacy. And it starts with how you approach your very next conversation.

Looking back over my career, I realize something interesting: the relationships that mattered most weren't defined by the titles on our business cards or the companies we worked for. They transcended all of that. When Jayson moved to different roles at Adobe, our relationship didn't change. When I switched companies, the genuine connections I'd built remained intact. That's because genuine relationships aren't tied to positions or organizations but to people. This has made me think a lot about legacy, not in terms of achievements or deals closed, but in terms of our lasting impact on each other's lives and careers. When I look at someone like Keith Ferrazzi, whom I talked about earlier, I see that his impact on my career wasn't just about what he taught me directly. It was about how his relationship approach influenced how I've built my network, approached my leadership roles, and tried to impact others.

I've noticed something about deep relationships in business: They create ripples that extend far beyond the original connection. The people I've built genuine relationships with go on to influence others in their networks, who influence others in turn. It's like dropping a stone in a pond–the ripples keep expanding outward. This isn't about networking or influence in the traditional sense. It's about how authentic relationships naturally create chains of trust and opportunity. When you build absolute trust with someone, they're more likely to extend that trust to others on your behalf. Not because you've asked them to, but because that's what genuine relationships do–they expand our circles of trust.

One of the most rewarding aspects of my career has been watching younger professionals I've worked with grow into leadership roles. Not because I mentored them in any formal way, but because we built genuine connections that allowed for real learning and growth in both directions. This has taught me something important about legacy: it's not about what you teach people directly. It's about the example you set in building and maintaining relationships. The junior account manager you treat with genuine respect today might be running their agency in five years. The intern you take the time to listen to might be a CMO a decade from now.

You can't approach relationships with this calculating, future-focused mindset. When you start thinking about people in terms of their future value, you've lost the authenticity that makes deep relationships possible. Actual legacy building happens when you treat every interaction and relationship as inherently valuable right now. I've had the privilege of working with professionals from multiple generations–from industry veterans who started their careers before digital marketing existed to Gen Z professionals who've never known a world without social media. Deep relationships can bridge these generational gaps in powerful ways. When you focus on building genuine connections rather than just professional networks, age and experience differences become less relevant. What matters is the authentic exchange of ideas, experiences, and perspectives. I've learned as much from twenty-something digital natives as I have from forty-year industry veterans precisely because I approached those relationships with genuine curiosity rather than preconceptions.

Yes, deep relationships can help you close deals and advance your career, but their real power lies in how they transform entire organizations and industries. Building genuine relationships across companies and roles creates informal networks of trust and collaboration that make entire industries work better. You create channels for knowledge sharing that benefit everyone. You build bridges between different parts of the business world that might otherwise remain disconnected.

Your life will be so much more rewarding if you approach building relationships not by trying to collect business cards or contacts but by really authentically caring about people and their stories, about who they are and what makes them tick, and about adding value at all levels of their professional and personal lives. You'll have the most amazing friends because the basis of your relationships is rooted first in generosity. You'll have many interesting people you can call, chat with, and get advice from. One of my favorite things about becoming an RV traveler is that while driving around the country, there's probably not a place I drive through where I don't flip through my mental Rolodex and find someone to connect with. Often, during COVID-19, especially, I showed up exactly when people needed someone–maybe during a divorce, after going to jail for fighting with their father-in-law, or during times of isolation. We'd spend days together, make milkshakes with my kids, and create new memories.

I might not be able to go to Bali and find somebody I know who lives there, but I can apply my relationship-building strategy. I can type into Google 'networking events in Bali,' go on Facebook events, find things to do, and put myself in situations where I don't have my guard up and am open to meeting new people. I can explore the world through the eyes of those who live there. I have an infinite and exhaustive list of things I want to do and people I want to see worldwide. Not only do those experiences add tremendous value to my life, but they also allow me to connect with those people more deeply at every touch point. It's not a strategy—it's a mindset, a way of living.

David Ogilvy fascinates me because he created "deep relationships" in advertising before anyone even had a term for it. In the 1960s, when everyone else was focused on the quick sale, Ogilvy told clients things they didn't want to hear. He'd turn down business if he thought a product wasn't good enough—imagine doing that today in the agency world. There's this famous story about Ogilvy working with Rolls-Royce. Instead of just writing flashy copy, he spent three weeks reading technical manuals and interviewing engineers. He drove their engineers crazy with questions. The result was the legendary headline: "At 60 miles an hour, the loudest noise in this new Rolls-Royce comes from the electric clock."

We're often tempted to take shortcuts in media and advertising. We can get hung up on follower counts and engagement rates. But Ogilvy understood something fundamental: you can't create authentic connections-- whether with clients or their customers-- without doing the deep work. What's interesting about Ogilvy is how his relationships compound over time. His relationship with American Express started in 1962. The agency still has that account today, decades after his death. Same with IBM, Dove, and others. He built relationships so deep that they outlived him. This leads to something I've been thinking about a lot lately. Our industry often measures success by quarterly results or campaign metrics. However, Ogilvy was playing a completely different game. He was building relationships that could span generations. He'd tell clients, "You're not buying our agency's time; you're buying our agency's brains and heart." That's an entirely different way of thinking about business relationships.

I was about hitting numbers, closing deals, and moving fast when I started. But what I've learned–and what Ogilvy demonstrated throughout his career–is that the real value comes from being willing to go deep, really understand your client's businesses, and care about their success more than your immediate gains. One of my other favorite Ogilvy stories is about a meeting where a client complained that he was behind schedule on some deliverables. Instead of making excuses, Ogilvy said, "Your business is so fascinating that I got carried away doing research. I'll pay for the delay out of my pocket." Who does that? But that's precisely the kind of thing that turns a business relationship into a partnership that can last decades.

The legacy Ogilvy left wasn't just about great advertising campaigns. It was about showing that when you prioritize deep understanding and genuine relationships over quick wins, you can build something beyond your career. I'm trying to develop relationships and understanding so deep that they create value long after I'm gone. Your legacy ultimately comes from consistently applying the going deep approach throughout your career—creating authentic connections, showing appropriate vulnerability, maintaining long-term orientation, generating mutual value, and being intentional about relationship depth. The relationships you build become a means to success and a significant part of success.

Research on what psychologists call "relationship currencies" provides a fascinating framework for understanding how business relationships evolve beyond transactional exchanges. Dr. Monica Worline and Dr. Jane Dutton at the University of Michigan identified five distinct currencies that flow through professional relationships: informational (sharing knowledge), developmental (helping others grow), resource (providing tangible assistance), political (lending influence), and emotional (offering personal support). Their research with executives across multiple industries found that relationships limited to one or two currencies—typically informational and resource-based—remained transactional. However, relationships incorporating three or more currencies naturally evolved into deeper connections that transcended organizational boundaries and roles. This explains why the most meaningful business relationships in my career have involved multiple dimensions of exchange beyond the immediate business purpose. When you share influence, emotional support, or developmental opportunities alongside business transactions, you fundamentally transform the nature of the relationship.

Learning from the best

Warren Buffett once remarked, "It takes 20 years to build a reputation and five minutes to ruin it." If you think about that, you'll do things differently. I learned this mindset from Keith Ferrazzi, the master of it.

Keith had a significant impact on my life early in my development as a professional, just through his intellectual property and his book, *Never Eat Alone*. I don't remember where I initially heard about that book. It may have been from another Sigma Chi member on the executive team in the LA Sigma Chi alum chapter. When I first read that book, it brought me to life. It created concrete examples of some of the things that I was starting to become familiar with through organic networking myself, like this idea that if you want to be successful in creating business relationships, you have to start from a place of generosity and what's in it for other people and putting good vibes into the world versus approaching relationship development of "What's in it for me?" Also, some of the very tactical components of concepts that he had, like "Conference Commando," which is a way to think about how to create a strategic plan and go to a conference with a plan in mind so you know who you want to meet and how you're going to meet all those people, or the idea of "Drafting," which is creating an event on top of an event.

If you go to a big trade show versus the conference itself, how do you create a minor satellite event that gets all the best people in the room so you don't have to go and run around a conference and meet all the people? You can monopolize the conference and get the people you want to meet to your event. That was a pretty interesting concept. Another lesson I think about is his concept of "Follow up or fail." So many people go out, meet, and network, but don't follow up. So, the most impressive people follow up the same night. If you go out networking and you follow up that same night before you get up the next morning, that can be impressive. I learned many great concepts from Keith's book and heard he was a Sigma Chi. I think there's a percentage of people who, when they read that book, no matter what, because it's about networking and building relationships, they inevitably find themselves wanting to reach out to him and build a relationship. I tried every way I could to figure it out: I tried to guess what his email address was, leveraged LinkedIn, and did everything to build a cold relationship.

Then I got connected to another Sigma Chi who had worked for him at some point, and I mentioned I was a fan of the book and that I would love to get the opportunity to meet him. That gentleman made an introduction, and Keith answered very quickly. That was another example: sometimes, going cold, you're just ramming up against a brick wall. But if you can find somebody who knows somebody you want to get to know, a referral, especially one from somebody they respect or have worked with or have a good relationship with–that referral goes a long way.

With that referral, Keith responded quickly, saying, "Hey, I would love to have you down to Barry's Bootcamp in West Hollywood and join me for a workout and brunch." I later learned, after attending that event, that I wasn't the only person Keith invited to work out. I was one of 10 people that morning who showed up to work out and then had brunch with him. Keith was in his forties then, muscular, tanned, well-dressed, and in fantastic shape. He achieved that by going to Barry's Bootcamp every day whenever he was in a city with a Barry's Bootcamp. And if he doesn't have access to Barry's Bootcamp, he works out with a personal trainer and does that every day except Sunday. six days a week. He's religious about his diet and workout schedule.

That was very impressive to me that somebody who had achieved some of the things that he had gained, like becoming the youngest partner in the history of Deloitte in his 20s and the youngest Fortune 500 chief marketing officer in history when he became the CMO of Starwood Hotels in his thirties, those were impressive feats. I certainly can't ever claim to be in anywhere near as good a shape as Keith was in his forties, but it did instill in me the importance of trying to get exercise and making that part of my wellness routine.

Getting to meet him in that first interaction was cool, as it was an opportunity to meet someone who had had such a significant impact on me through his intellectual property and book. Getting to meet him at a workout and then going to hang out for coffee at brunch afterward, and then I found out a few years later, when I went to work for him, that that was something that he not only did on Saturdays but did every day of the week and was just kind of a very cool entry-level way of getting to know and meet new people. Outside of exercise, Keith always wore a suit with a powder blue shirt and no tie, so that was his professional dress. It was a suit with a blue shirt and no tie. And he would drink unsweetened iced tea. That was his beverage of choice.

Because I became part of the company and was in a business development role, it was an open-door policy for me to go and hang out and work out with him anytime I wanted, so I did that fairly often. I got to the point where I would go to that workout, not even to spend time and have face time with Keith anymore, because I was working for him. I would go there to network because you never knew who would attend one of these networking events. Over time, I got invited to other things like dinner parties and cocktail parties at his house or conferences like the Big Task weekend that he would do in Pasadena. Another thing that I appreciated about Keith was that he would blend community service into the workplace before it was fashionable. We would have a few touchpoints of the year where we would go out and volunteer for an organization called Kids Save. We would go out and hang out with some foster kids from the LA area, spend time with them, and give them attention.

Keith was an innovator who did not see the whole experience of giving back as essential for company culture. Still, he also saw it as an accelerator for relationship development. Everything was tactical regarding how he could cement the relationships inside his organization and with external stakeholders. If you're on a mission and you're serving with your colleagues, or even your prospects or customers, shoulder to shoulder, you're out there in the trenches doing good work and giving back to the community. That's another way to accelerate relationships drastically. Look for opportunities to volunteer and give back to your local community. Moreover, you can go on a mission trip-style environment where you spend time volunteering together in the trenches and helping people. In that case, that's also a great way to accelerate relationships. So Keith was an innovator there. Now, every corporation has a giveback policy or a way that they give back and support nonprofits and volunteer for a day of service or something like that, but he did that before it was a trendy thing.

The most interesting part of getting to work for Keith was the bittersweet reality that he was the first person who ever fired me as well. He was not an easy person to work for. And that's the danger of idolizing thought leaders and people whose material you read. You end up forming a relationship with them, or a business partnership, or, in my case, getting to work for someone who was one of your all-time business heroes at some point in your life. The reality is, when you read about somebody, you're getting the best version of them. You're getting the shiny, varnished way they want to be presented to the world. And the reality is, we're all human beings.

One of the things that I remember most about Keith was when I would accompany him on business trips, and we would go to dinner. He would ask funny and outrageous questions from time to time, like, "Oh, do you cheat on your wife?" It was done mainly in jest, but what he was always trying to do was just try to go deep and find ways to learn more about what makes you tick and who you are. But almost a part of him wanted to know your secrets, to ingratiate himself by getting you to tell him things that you wouldn't tell anybody else. I was careful in that regard. I didn't go as deep as I could have in giving him details about my personal life. I don't know why, but I never felt comfortable going there with him.

On one of our first business trips, I was just so excited that I was getting to travel professionally for the first time. Keith was inviting me to dinner because we're in the same hotel, and he was running training, and then I'm training him for a smaller group of people after he leaves. I came to dinner expecting to enjoy and get to know him better. Then he ripped me a new one for not bringing my prospect list and using our time together to make it a working dinner. He taught me a good lesson: You should always be prepared, and when you have those moments with your senior leadership, you should use those moments wisely, come prepared, and use that time.

But I also felt bad for him that he felt like every interaction: his workouts are all networking events, and every party he hosts for dinner is somehow biz dev. It made me feel like his life might be exhausting. Maybe that's just me rationalizing and making excuses for the fact that as good as I think I am at networking and business development, I can never quite live up to the expectations or the model that Keith had set personally, just as far as how many relationships he was able to manage, how deep he was able to go with those individuals. However, the amount of time he puts in day after day, night after night, and weekend after weekend was impressive, but it was also not something I ever felt like I wanted to emulate completely. I need balance to enjoy my life and time with my family.

Keith could hold his own with the best of them, chewing you out and making you feel bad for messing up. However, it always felt like it was done from a place where he wanted to push you to be better, more prepared, work harder, and work faster. I vividly remember one early morning workout at Barry's Bootcamp. The red lights of the studio cast everyone in the same dramatic glow, sweat already forming on foreheads as we prepared for the grueling session ahead. Despite being in his forties, Keith outpaced nearly everyone in the room, pushing through sprints on the treadmill with an impressive and intimidating focused intensity.

After the workout, we gathered at a nearby coffee shop. The air conditioning was a welcome relief as we sat at a long wooden table, protein shakes in hand. That morning, there were five of us—three potential clients, another colleague, and me. I was still new to working with Keith, trying to understand the unwritten rules.

"So, Dylan," Keith said suddenly, turning his attention to me. "What's your follow-up plan with everyone here?"

The question caught me off guard. I stumbled through a vague answer about scheduling individual meetings.

Keith's expression shifted, not to anger but to disappointment. "That's amateur hour," he said, his voice low but intense. "You should already have the next steps planned for each person before we even finish our drinks."

Embarrassed, my face flushed hot as I felt everyone's eyes on me. But then, Keith did something unexpected. He turned it into a teaching moment.

"Here's how it should work," he said, addressing everyone. "Dylan should have researched each of you thoroughly enough to know exactly what value he can offer next. For Mark, that might be an introduction to someone in his target industry. For Sarah, maybe it's sharing a specific case study relevant to her current challenge."

He continued outlining a level of preparation and strategic thinking that hadn't occurred to me. It was embarrassing at the moment, but also a master class in relationship building.

Later that day, Keith called me. I braced myself for more criticism, but his tone had changed completely.

"You know why I pushed you this morning?" he asked.

"Because I wasn't prepared," I responded.

"No," he said. "Because you're capable of much more. When I call someone out, it's because I see potential they're not fulfilling yet."

That moment transformed our relationship and my approach to networking. Keith wasn't just demanding perfection—he was demonstrating what genuine investment in professional relationships looks like. It's not about collecting contacts or making superficial connections. It's about showing up fully prepared to add specific value to each person you interact with.

I didn't lose sight of the irony that this lesson in deep relationship building came through a moment of public correction. But that was Keith's genius—he didn't just teach principles through books and talks. He created situations where the lessons became visceral and unforgettable.

Working with Keith wasn't always comfortable, but it was always valuable. He showed me that going deep in business relationships isn't just about being friendly—it's about caring enough to push others to their potential, even when that means having difficult conversations. While working for him, I saw Keith in action many times, including when he hosted long, "slow dinners." He would gather executives outside the office and boardroom around a dinner table to break bread, just getting people out of a professional environment and into a personal one.

What Keith would do in the process of these long, slow dinners was facilitate conversation. This works way better at a dinner at home, in an Airbnb, or where there are none of the typical distractions of being at a restaurant, where there are many people around who could hear what the conversation is, a lot of dishes clanging, and other noises. It works best when you're in an isolated situation. Keith was the master of facilitating questions that allowed people to be vulnerable. It didn't necessarily incite vulnerability, but it allowed them to be authentic and talk about real things that were going on in their lives. An example of a question he would ask (and keep in mind the people that got invited to Keith's dinners were generally not schlubs-- these are all big executives, prominent type-A alpha personalities), he would go around the table and ask, "What's the most impactful thing that happened to you in the last week?"

Sometimes, you would get an alpha-type person to jump into the conversation and say something cringy like, "Oh, man, it was such a great week. I closed a hundred-million-dollar deal, I flew my private jet to Vegas, and blah blah blah." It was just a douchey peacock--a braggy showcase. That doesn't do anything but repel and disgust people. It is surprising that a person like that could even be as successful as they are.

Nonetheless, you would always get one of those guys in the mix, but what would invariably happen is you would land on somebody who had something significant happen in their life.

I remember one particular dinner at Keith's home in the Hollywood Hills. The space created a sense of intimacy, with warm lighting from artfully placed lamps. This long wooden table somehow made everyone feel connected rather than distant, and floor-to-ceiling windows transformed the twinkling Los Angeles skyline into a dramatic backdrop for our conversation.

Eight of us sat around the table that night—two venture capitalists, a tech CEO, a marketing executive, a nonprofit leader, Keith, me, and another colleague. The food was deliberately served slowly, each course becoming sustenance and a marker for a new level of conversation.

Keith opened with his signature question: "What's the most impactful thing that happened to you last week?"

The first few responses were predictable—professional victories, business challenges overcome, the typical currency of executive conversation. Then came Mark's turn. He was the tech CEO known for his aggressive growth strategies and take-no-prisoners approach to competition. Everyone expected another success story.

Instead, his voice softened. "My son tried to run away this week," he said, his fingers nervously tracing the rim of his wine glass. "He's sixteen, adopted, and struggling with identity issues we don't know how to help with."

The energy in the room shifted instantly. The subtle competitive vibe that had underscored earlier sharing disappeared. Mark continued, gradually revealing more about his family challenges, his voice occasionally breaking with emotion. He talked about feeling like a failure as a parent despite his business success, about the late-night conversations with his wife about whether they were equipped to handle their son's needs.

"I don't know why I'm sharing all this," he said finally, looking up with a half-embarrassed smile. "I haven't even told my board I took yesterday off to meet with therapists."

What happened next was remarkable. The venture capitalist across the table, who had earlier boasted about a successful exit, leaned forward. "My daughter struggled with similar issues," he said quietly. "It was the hardest period of our lives."

One by one, these highly accomplished individuals began sharing their vulnerabilities—health scares, relationship struggles, personal doubts—things that would never emerge in boardrooms or conference calls. The marketing executive talked about her recent divorce. The nonprofit leader spoke about his father's dementia.

I watched Keith during all this, noting how he barely spoke but somehow orchestrated the sharing with subtle nods, attentive listening, and perfectly timed questions that deepened the conversation without forcing it.

These former strangers exchanged phone numbers over

dessert and planned to continue their conversations privately. They weren't networking anymore—they were connecting as humans who recognized something of themselves in each other's struggles.

Afterward, as I walked out to my car, Keith stepped beside me. "That's how real business relationships are built," he said simply. "Not through exchanging capabilities, but through exchanging humanity."

That dinner taught me something profound about deepening business relationships. When we create spaces where honest human sharing can happen—where the professional masks can safely come off, even temporarily—we build connections that transcend typical business boundaries. Those relationships become resilient in ways that purely professional connections never can.

I've incorporated this approach in my relationship building, creating environments where authentic sharing feels natural rather than forced. It doesn't require elaborate dinners in the Hollywood Hills. It can happen over coffee, during a walk, or even in brief moments of genuine interest in someone else's life. The key is creating psychological safety and demonstrating that you value the whole person, not just their business utility.

Thoughts on mentorship

From the perspective of open networking, I accept all inbound requests on LinkedIn. Generally, if you can track down my phone number and leave a compelling voicemail, I'll probably answer it. If you send me a text or email, I'm pretty accessible via social media or traditional channels. The thing that I'm always looking for, which most executives are, is to show me that you're looking to add value first.

Research me and understand the things that make me tick. If you invite me out to play golf, play pickleball, have a cigar, or even offer me lunch or a coffee, 9 times out of 10, I'll say yes. I like free coffee. I enjoy a free lunch. Those other things I mentioned add even more value to me, but generally, when somebody reaches out to me because they want to meet in person. They want to add value or offer something generous, even a $5 cup of coffee. If I have space in my calendar, you might have to wait a week or two, but I'll meet up with you. Still, I operate from the perspective that you just never know where a relationship will come from as long as you reach out from the perspective of generosity.

I recently had a Sigma Chi reach out to me who was a financial services guy, and sadly, I just told them, "Look, a lot of Sigma Chis have reached out to me over the years that want to manage my money, and the reality is that I'm a self-directed investor. My wife manages our money. We don't work with third parties."

And then he said, "Hey, man, hold on! Hold on! I'm just contacting you because we've connected on LinkedIn. We're fellow Sigma Chis, and I will be in San Diego. I wanted to know if you wanted to join us for a round of golf."

And then I said, "Okay." Sometimes, I have to check myself. We're all inundated and bombarded with so many inbound requests and marketing messages and automated AI chatbot outreach, people from overseas–not that I have anything against people from overseas. Still, we all get the inbound requests that are never led from a perspective of adding value, reading with generosity, or leading with proof that you've done your homework. Those are very easy to ignore, so hit the delete button. Unsubscribe.

Do a few minutes of homework, write something that's custom-tailored that would show me that you know the things that move the needle for me, either professionally or personally, that make me tick, lead with generosity, and 9 times out of 10, I'll probably meet you halfway and want to form a relationship and see how I can be helpful to you. I have mixed personal experiences and opinions about the formal idea of mentorship. I've never had a formal mentor, and I say that with a bit of sadness. I've had the opportunity to work for some fantastic human beings. I have already jotted down the list: Howard Bragman, the founder of Bragman Nyman Cafarelli; Bruce Nash, a top reality television producer; and Keith Ferrazzi. When I went into the sales world, I saw people like Pat McKenna, the founder of Strike Social, and Tony Chen at Channel Factory. For whatever reason, I've been transactional in those relationships and added a lot of value when we worked together. But then, when I move on, I like to have closure, and I want to put that chapter in my life to bed and not revisit it as much.

This raises an essential point about mentorship in the context of going deep. True mentorship isn't about collecting wisdom from someone higher up the ladder—it's about creating a relationship with enough depth that both parties invest in each other's growth. In my experience, the most valuable mentoring relationships aren't formally labeled as such but evolve naturally from authentic connections.

The idea that you're going to go out and send somebody an email or find somebody who will sign up as your mentor, so to speak, is far-fetched. Actual mentorships and authentic relationships come from having that superior-subordinate relationship within a corporate environment. There are good managers and good bosses and not-so-great bosses and managers.

I've observed that the most impactful mentorship relationships emerge from a foundation of mutual respect and genuine connection. They're rarely established through cold outreach or formal programs. Instead, they develop when two people recognize something in each other—a shared value system, complementary skills, or aligned ambitions— and choose to invest in that connection beyond the immediate transaction. Suppose I look at myself, even though I've moved out of being an individual contributor in sales and moved into more sales leadership. In that case, the management style I've always appreciated and like to mentor is teaching by example. Anytime one of my sales reps wants me to go with them to a meeting or a call, as long as I'm available, I'm always down to jump on the phone and do the sales pitch with them. I also take over sales meetings, so many reps can get over that pretty fast when I dominate their meetings and structure because I just can't help myself.

I've learned that mentoring others is not enough to simply tell someone what to do or how to do it. The most impactful mentorship happens when you invite others into your process, letting them see how you think, handle difficult situations, and build relationships. This kind of transparency creates opportunities for deeper learning beyond skills, including mindset and approach. An essential component of being a good mentor is having an open-door policy where you're available and they can ask questions. My job as a manager is to remove internal obstacles so they can thrive in their role, get them the resources needed to be effective salespeople, and advocate on their behalf. The other way that I've always tried to mentor and lead is by getting out of people's way, not over-micromanaging them, not overburdening them with internal meetings and sales training and things to do, but giving them a wide berth and treating them as a responsible adult, and that they can go out and get the job done that they need to do with as little oversight as possible.

This approach to mentorship aligns perfectly with the principles of going deep. Rather than creating dependency, it fosters autonomy while providing support. It recognizes that the person being mentored isn't just looking to extract knowledge but to develop professionally. This requires vulnerability from both sides—the mentor must be willing to show their imperfections and uncertainties, while the mentee must be open about their challenges and ambitions. And to my failings, I've lost people, especially from the Gen Z and millennial spectrum, coming out of college and helicopter parenting style relationships, where they expect a lot of structure out of their career and their job. When coming through the entertainment industry and the early days of media, we weren't given much other than an email address or a telephone. It was like, "Here you go, go out there and figure this stuff out on your own." I may be a bit jaded, and I come from the perspective of sink or swim.

I've had to adapt my approach to mentoring as different generations enter the workforce. What worked for me doesn't always work for everyone else. The deeper I go into my relationships with team members, the more I recognize that effective mentorship isn't one-size-fits-all. Some people thrive with independence and minimal structure, while others need more frequent touchpoints and explicit guidance. Going deep as a mentor means understanding these individual needs and adapting your approach accordingly. In terms of thinking about mentorships or seeking out mentors, it's organic. It generally happens as a byproduct of your professional relationships. The idea that you're going to go out and find someone who isn't family, or somehow otherwise invested in your ultimate success as an outsider that doesn't have that vested interest in you either as a family member or a subordinate, I think it's hard to get that level of engagement from someone senior to you. Because what is it ultimately that you're invested in? Outside of a corporate structure, it's harder to find those relationships.

However, I've come to believe that mentorship doesn't always have to come from above. Some of the most valuable mentoring I've received has come from peers and even people who technically reported to me. When we expand our definition of mentorship beyond the traditional hierarchical model, we open ourselves to learning opportunities from every direction. This is particularly true in sales, where the landscape is constantly evolving. Sometimes, the newest team member has insights about digital platforms or emerging trends from which even the most seasoned veterans can learn.

I've also found that mentorship doesn't have to be a single, comprehensive relationship with one person. Instead, I've developed a "mentorship portfolio"—different people I learn from in other areas. One person might be exceptional at relationship building, another at negotiation tactics, and yet another at strategic thinking. I've developed a more rounded perspective by going deep with multiple mentors in specific domains rather than seeking one all-encompassing mentor. For those seeking mentorship, focus less on finding a formal mentor and more on identifying people whose specific strengths you admire. Approach them with curiosity rather than expectation. Ask focused questions about their approach to particular challenges rather than asking them to "be your mentor." This specificity makes it easier for them to help you and makes it more likely that they'll invest in the relationship.

The most powerful mentoring relationships I've observed share a common characteristic: reciprocity. Even with significant differences in experience or position, both parties must bring value to the relationship. As a mentee, you offer fresh perspectives, technical knowledge, or the energizing effect of your curiosity and growth. The best mentorships evolve into partnerships where both people feel they're getting as much as they're giving. This reciprocity is the essence of going deep in mentorship. It transforms what could be a transactional exchange of information into a genuine relationship where both parties are invested in each other's success. When this happens, the mentorship transcends its original purpose. It becomes more enduring—a relationship that creates value for both people long after their roles change.

In the end, whether you're seeking mentorship or offering it to others, the principles we've explored throughout this book apply. Lead with generosity, focus on the relationship rather than the transaction, create a foundation of trust and mutual respect, and be willing to go beyond surface-level interactions to create something significant. When mentorship is approached this way, it becomes one of the most potent expressions of going deep in business.

The future of deep relationships

The future isn't about replacing human connection with technology. It's about using technology to make more space for human connection. Every minute saved by automation is a minute you can spend in a real conversation. Every task AI handles is mental energy you can devote to understanding someone's needs and challenges. This isn't just philosophical—it's practical. In a world where everyone tries to automate relationships, genuine human connection becomes even more valuable.

As we look to the future, I see challenges and opportunities for building deep business relationships. Technology is changing how we connect; remote work is changing how we interact, and younger generations are bringing new expectations and communication styles to the business world. But the fundamental truth remains: authentic human connection is irreplaceable. Building genuine, trust-based relationships becomes even more valuable as our world becomes more digital and automated. It becomes a key differentiator in a world where surface-level connections are easy, but deep relationships are rare.

Throughout this book, we've explored what it means to go deep in business relationships—to move beyond transactional interactions toward authentic human connections characterized by mutual trust, understanding, and value creation. We've seen how the five elements of going deep—authentic connection, appropriate vulnerability, long-term orientation, mutual value creation, and intentional depth—transform not just individual relationships but entire approaches to business development.

<u>Key principles that can transform your approach to sales and business development:</u>

- *Authenticity trumps technique*: People respond to genuine human connection more than polished sales tactics. The most substantial business relationships are built on the same foundations

as personal ones—trust, mutual respect, and shared experiences.
- *Depth beats volume*: Rather than spreading yourself thin with hundreds of superficial connections, focus your energy on deepening relationships with strategic contacts. The A/B/C framework I've outlined provides a practical way to manage this approach.
- *Vulnerability creates opportunity*: Appropriate openness accelerates relationship building. Showing your authentic self, within professional boundaries, creates space for others to do the same, establishing deeper connections.
- *Balance technology and humanity*: Use digital tools to handle the logistics of relationship maintenance, but never as a substitute for genuine human interaction. Technology should create space for deeper connection, not replace it.
- *Create value before expecting returns*: Approach every relationship with generosity first. When you focus on how you can help others succeed, the returns often exceed your expectations.

The future belongs to those building meaningful connections in an increasingly digital world. As AI continues to automate routine tasks and communications, your ability to create genuine human relationships becomes your most significant competitive advantage. It can't be replicated by algorithms or outsourced to technology.

. . .

Your Call to Action:

- *Start today*: Identify one key relationship in your network that deserves more depth. Reach out—not with a business agenda but with genuine curiosity about their challenges and opportunities.
- *Audit your network*: Apply the A/B/C framework to your current connections. Be honest about where you invest your relationship energy and whether that aligns with your long-term goals.
- *Create space for depth*: Block time on your calendar for relationship building. This isn't just networking—it's an intentional investment in the connections that will sustain your career.
- *Practice appropriate vulnerability*: In your next business conversation, share something slightly more personal than you usually would (within professional boundaries). Notice how this shifts the dynamic.
- *Build your legacy consciously*: Consider what relationship legacy you want to leave. How do you want people to describe working with you? What lasting impact do you want to have on others' careers and lives?

THE DEEP APPROACH isn't always the easiest path. It requires more initial investment, greater emotional intelligence, and consistent attention. But as we've explored through countless examples and practical strategies, it creates increasingly valuable and self-sustaining relationships over time.

Remember the story of my relationship with Jayson at Adobe—what began as a LinkedIn connection evolved into family vacations and millions in revenue over eight years. That relationship wasn't built through clever sales techniques or aggressive follow-up. It was formed through genuine connection, consistent value creation, and a willingness to invest in the relationship beyond business outcomes.

You can create those kinds of transformative relationships in your career. Not just one, but many—a network of deep connections that sustain you through market fluctuations, career transitions, and business challenges. Ultimately, your legacy isn't measured in deals closed or revenue generated. It's measured in the strength and depth of the relationships you've built and how they continue to create value and opportunity for others long after your direct involvement has ended. Your journey toward more profound, more meaningful business relationships starts now. Not with dramatic changes to your approach but with small, intentional shifts in how you view, build, and nurture your professional connections. This book has given you the insights and tools to begin that journey. I'd love to hear about your experiences as you implement these ideas. Connect with me on LinkedIn to share your stories of going deep, or invite me for a coffee meeting. Who knows, maybe we'll become friends.

ABOUT THE AUTHOR

Dylan Conroy is a revenue leader and relationship builder who has generated over $50 million in advertising and media sales throughout his 15-year career. He has held senior positions at major agencies and tech companies, including Channel Factory and The Social Standard. Based in San Diego, Dylan hosts a popular business podcast on marketing and revenue leadership. He lives with his wife, Myla, and their three children—the "Triple T's": Teegan, Tennyson, and Tristan.

Nathan Pettijohn is an author and entrepreneur. Nathan is a contributing writer for Forbes on topics relating to what business leaders need to know about innovations in media and technology. Nathan is also the author of a travelogue called *Travels With Hafa,* and two fiction novels, *Public Opinion* and *For What It's Worth*. In 2011, Nathan founded Cordurouy, a digital strategy agency based in Los Angeles where he serves as CEO. He resides somewhere in Central or South America with his dog, Raphael.

www.ingramcontent.com/pod-product-compliance
Lightning Source LLC
Chambersburg PA
CBHW062106080426
42734CB00012B/2765